LETTING
OFF
STEAM

(52 Thoughts For
52 Weeks)

A CIP catalogue record for this book is available from
the British Library.

Printed and bound in Great Britain.

Paper used in the production of books published by
United Press comes only from sustainable forests.

ISBN 978-1-84436-818-1

First published in Great Britain in 2008 by
United Press Ltd
Admail 3735
London
EC1B 1JB
Tel: 0870 240 6190
Fax: 0870 240 6191
ISBN for complete set of volumes
978-1-84436-528-9
All Rights Reserved

© Copyright Leslie Scrase 2009

www.unitedpress.co.uk

SOME PREVIOUS BOOKS
by
Leslie Scrase

Booklet On Anglican/Methodist Conversations

Some Ancestors Of Humanism

Conversations Between An Atheist And A
Christian
(A Study Of Matthew's Gospel)

Coping With Death
(3rd Edition)

THE AUTHOR

Leslie Scrase grew up in Surrey, Sussex and North Devon where he was evacuated during the Second World War.

After National Service in the Royal Navy he became a minister of religion. Over a period of twenty years he worked in various parts of the United Kingdom and in Southern India.

After the loss of his Christian Faith he became a Humanist Celebrant working in Surrey and Dorset for over thirty years.

Twice married, he and Wendy share six children and twenty one grand-children so far. At the time of writing the first of two great grand-children were expected!

DEDICATION

To Friendship.

Many of my long-standing friends have
unwittingly contributed to these pages by
forcing me to think!
Let me mention a few by name:

David and Betty Allen.
Margaret Davis.
Two unknown Christians, One Indian and
One English.
Audrey Platt.
John and Barbara Eedle.

These are but a few amongst many.

Epicurus wrote:

'Friendship goes dancing round the world,
proclaiming to us all to awake to the
praises of a happy life.'

PREFACE

The British Humanist Association staff were not very pleased. Once again the powers that be at the BBC had decided that it was not possible to include humanists in their "Thought For The Day" slot.

Apparently thought, like morals, is the preserve of religious people. Those of us who are not religious are thoroughly immoral and are incapable of thought.

Far be it from me to argue with that!

And yet from time to time other people's thoughts stir me into a reaction of my own. They have made me think - except of course for the fact that as an atheist I am incapable of thought.

Sometimes my reactions have been published and sometimes I have published them myself in my newsletters and magazines. Because the BBC will never use any of them I am not tied either to time or length. But the thought came to me - no, I'm forgetting. Thoughts are not possible. The idea perhaps? Oh! I don't know. Anyway, I decided to gather together 52 thoughts for the year (one for every week), once described by John Bushell as "The Ramblings Of A Crank!"

Leslie Scrase

CONTENTS

Preface

Dedication

WEEK 1

A New Calendar

Pristine, pure, clean and almost empty. There are one or two things carried forward from the old year to spoil its purity. And that's the problem isn't it.

When a new baby is born it has that same pristine purity. Although it carries forward with it a great deal from its parents it is nonetheless, unstained and perfect. (As you will gather, I don't believe any of this 'original sin' business that Christians prattle on about. I never did, even when I was a Christian.)

But we are no longer babies, so we DO carry baggage forward with us into the New Year. I read recently, "A new Calendar does not make a new man." More's the pity - or is it?

Do we need to be new or changed? Or is it that the old model just needs tweaking a little bit here and there?

I doubt if any of us are TOTALLY dissatisfied with what we are. In a recent poem I found myself writing:

> The child is father to the man.
> The young is father to the old.
> I was, I am and I'm content
> With most of all that I've become.

"Most?" Since I wrote it I've wondered about that. Is it perhaps a bit too cocky? And am I content with me as I am? Not entirely, that's for sure.

I imagine that most people would say the same. So what are we going to do about it? Are we going to make New Year's Resolutions?

I suspect that that is something we should approach with caution. When I was a young man I bought a small book of devotion. At the back of the book were pages for my own devotions and there was a page for my vows. On that page I wrote:

"If I make none, I break none."

I was wiser than I knew. Certainly at the other end of my life I can look back and say sadly that I have broken most of the vows I ever made.

So, perhaps we should be careful not to ask too much of ourselves. On the other hand wasn't it Kipling who told us that we should aim high because, if we aim high and miss by a little we still achieve more than if we aim low and achieve our goal.

Perhaps if we mingle realism, optimism and determination we shall not go too far wrong. We may not prove to be winners in the race of life but we can aim to put in a fairly creditable performance.

WEEK 2

Belief, Knowledge and Imagination

People sometimes ask me what I believe.

When I was younger I would always try to answer them. Nowadays I tend to push the question back to them:

"If you really want to know what I think, I'll tell you, but it seems to me that where I stand is of no importance except to me. What really matters is what YOU think. What DO you think?"

They nearly always try to answer and I end up not having to answer the question at all.

As a matter of fact, it was that question which led me on my long pilgrimage away from Christianity. I had been preaching in Medak Cathedral in South India. Afterwards an elderly local man came home with me for a coffee and to talk about my sermon.

"But what do YOU believe?" he asked.
"I've just been telling you," I replied.

"No, he said, you've been telling me what the Bible says and what the Church says. But what do you believe?"

Twelve years later I knew the answer. Put as simply and bluntly as I can, I <u>believe</u> nothing!

It seems that we operate on two levels. One is the level of our knowledge. This is often pretty slight and often flawed. As a friend of mine once said,
"When I was twenty I knew all the answers. When I was forty, I knew all the questions. By the time I was sixty, I

couldn't remember either."

For someone my age I know very little, but it is enough to live by. Most of the time I know all that I need to know and when I don't know there will either be a hopelessly complicated book of instructions or there will be someone else with the knowledge I lack.

For the whole of my daily life I operate on the level of human knowledge. Nothing else is necessary.

The other level on which we operate is the level of the imagination. As far as I am concerned, every belief system, every religion is a matter of the human imagination and nothing more.

Imagination enriches us. It brings colour and light into our lives. It carries us off into flights of fancy, gives us pleasure, fun, excitement and occasionally, just occasionally it leads us to make intuitive leaps which lead to greater knowledge.

Where religion brings joy, it does so in the same way as drama does. It brings colour, light, music and companionship, but, it rarely brings knowledge.

It is when religion believes that it *knows* that it becomes dangerous,and it is when religious attitudes of *knowing* spill over into other areas of life that it brings danger to them too.

When religious people think that they *know* they become dogmatic and their *knowledge* becomes divisive. This leads to pain, suffering and conflict. These *knowers* always insist that they are right, no matter how many people disagree with them, and no matter how flawed the information on which they base their *knowledge*.

If I were asked who are the most dangerous people in the world today my answer would include a number of people who always seem to think that they are right beginning with the Pope. They operate, not on the basis of knowledge but on the basis of dogmatic assertion. I used to know the Chairman of a major British company whose method of debate was to shout louder than anyone else until he had battered them into silence. Their silence then proved he was right!

When religion says that it operates on the basis of **faith** that is fair enough, but when it claims to *know*, it claims too much.

As for me I am perfectly happy to allow my imagination free play and to shoot off in flights of fancy wherever my imagination likes to take me.

But for the affairs of everyday life I operate solely on the basis of the little I know. For daily living knowledge is everything.

WEEK 3

What Difference Does Your Religion Make?

Other people's questions have often been the stimulus I have needed. I have already mentioned the most crucial one of all: "What do YOU believe?"

It was in the years when I was slowly moving towards the answer to that question that I went to a meeting in Nottingham. During the meeting we were divided into groups and the group leader invited each of us to try to answer the question "What difference does your religion make?"

It was another question which was to bug me.

Modern Christianity seems to have lost its love for language but in those days the language used in churches was often very beautiful. So religion fed my love for language.

It also fed my love for singing and for music, although it has to be said that much of my own experience of church music was in small chapels where the sounds were pretty awful - I often felt that God must wear ear-muffs - and especially on occasions when there was no organist and I stepped into the breach.

Supremely the church was a place where good friendships could be made and some of those friendships have sustained me throughout my life. It was a place where you could find human nature at its best.

What I discovered as a Christian minister was that the church was also a place where you could find human nature at its worst and that seemed to deny everything the church stood for and to destroy everything it claimed for itself.

As I thought about the question I had been asked it became clear that I didn't need religion to feed my love for language, and I didn't need religion to feed my love for music, and I didn't need religion to enable me to form friendships.

So I pursued the question further. Many religious people claim that their religion gives them a direct, personal relationship with their God. I still claimed that for myself, but did it? What does 'a direct, personal relationship' with something that doesn't exist really mean?

When I asked 'what difference does your religion make,' I slowly came to the conclusion that it didn't make any practical difference to my life at all except that through it, I was spending a huge amount of time in useless pursuits. I probably still do, but at least I choose those pursuits for myself.

In practical terms I did not need my religion. I could get along perfectly well without it.

When I actually did, I felt as if a huge weight had been taken off my shoulders, life had become stress free. I remember a man once saying to me what a relief it was for him to be taken prisoner of war! For him war was over. I felt the same way and I shared Dean Inge's feelings:

"Perhaps the most lasting pleasure in life is the pleasure of not going to church."

Language, music, friendship, the direct, personal relationship with real people, these things remain and have often been enhanced.

When a hermit crab outgrows its shell-home it finds a larger shell to live in. Moving from one to another places it in danger, but when the move has been safely accomplished it can go on growing. I outgrew the shell of my religion and I like to think that I am still growing.

WEEK 4

Put Down None

When Cole Porter was dying he was admitted to hospital. A member of staff filled out the usual admittance form:

"Religion?"

Cole Porter replied, "Put down none."

The member of staff obviously found that difficult and asked if that meant "Protestant?"

But Cole Porter was adamant.

When I joined the Navy to do my National Service we were divided into three categories: Church Of England, Roman Catholic and Other Denominations. There was no room for *none* here. The Chaplain for Other Denominations wanted to know precisely which denomination we belonged to. We lined up and stood before him. My turn came:

"Religion?"

"Methodist."

Behind me a young Irish jockey was listening carefully.

"Religion?"

"Methylated."

I don't think the Navy was as hard on those who had no religion as the Army. There were certainly a few aetheists who never went on Church Parades although they had to *work-ship*, fulfilling other minor duties instead.

But it was certainly much harder then and in 1964 when Cole Porter was dying, to answer the question *Religion?* with *none.*

Yet there are still times when it is necessary to repeat the answer before people will put it down. Some people just can't accept that many of us (perhaps as many as 40%) have no religious beliefs whatsoever. So let me make it quite clear. If you ask me now, "What is your religion?" I shall answer with Cole Porter,

"Put down none."

WEEK 5

All at Sea

Many years ago I wrote a book expounding the *Nicene Creed*. I began to seek a publisher. When the Lutterworth Press rejected it for publication, they praised its orthodoxy and said that they were sure I would find a publisher. When I left the Church I threw it away together with three dustbins full of sermons and talks!
Much more recently I published my book "Conversations between an Atheist and a Christian." One member of the local clergy was kind enough to review it. I was amused when she criticised the Christian for his lack of knowledge of the *latest trends in theology*. His old fashioned orthodoxy obviously didn't suit her.

But I found myself wondering what those latest trends are and how many Christians are aware of them. The latest trends in my Christian days were the sort of things taught by the *death of God* theologians and the early *Sea Of Faith* theologians.

The latter have continued to influence many Christians who are desperate to cling on to their Christianity yet who have no real belief in the creeds they recite Sunday by Sunday. Religion was so much easier for people when I was a boy. Catholic Christians accepted the authority of the Church and Protestant Christians accepted the authority of the Bible (still given fairly literal acceptance.)

But for most Christians in this country those days are gone. They are lost in a sea of uncertainty and sail on through a fog of mystical vagueness. It often seems to me that in their desperation to cling on to some of the wreckage of the old religion, they are likely to drown.

In these post-religious days we each have to learn that the only way to a safe haven is for us to do our own swimming. That may be much harder than following a leader or obeying the dictates of some teacher, but it is the only really ADULT way to go.

WEEK 6

A bias to the right

Nine out of ten people are right handed. Eight out of ten people are right footed. Yet, astonishingly, most of the recent Presidents of the USA have been left handed: One of the Bush's, Bill Clinton, Gerald Ford and Ronald Regan and both of the candidates for the 2008 Presidential Election, Obama and McCain! (that should worry anyone who is left-handed.)

None of those presidents has done anything to redress the world's balance against left-handed people. Our technology from cheque books to scissors is all designed for right-handed people. As Lyall Watson pointed out in his book *Dark Nature* we show a consistent and predictable bias towards the right in almost everything, (including politics.)

Language underlines this bias against left-handedness. As a boy my friends called me *clicky handed* or *cack-handed* meaning awkward. (Unfortunately I justified the terms.) The French and Germans also think of left-handedness as awkward: gauche, linkisch and Spanish goes one step further: zurdo from azurdos means *to go the wrong way*. From this it is not far to the Romany bongo meaning crooked or fixed or the Latin sinister, a word which needs no translation.

But we don't need to look to other languages. Our own is full of expressions which warn us about the left: I don't know where I got these statements from but:

a left-handed compliment is an insult;

a left-handed diagnosis is wrong;

a child born on the left side or even leaning to left is either illegitimate or homosexual (which introduces us to two more groups who have suffered far more than us left-handers from religious and human prejudice;)

a left-handed deal is almost certainly crooked and best avoided;

and a left-handed wife is a mistress.

My mother was compelled to learn to write with her right hand (my grandfather even throwing the ink pot at her when she was using her left hand.)

I remember an educationalist expressing the opinion that left-handed children were always at a disadvantage in the classroom. Because I'm left-handed myself I was happy to use that statement to my own advantage. But isn't it time that the world of right-handed people gave the rest of us a square deal? After all left-handedness is also said "to be a sign of genius!"

Trivial? Too trivial to bother about? Perhaps. On the other hand, it may come as a gentle reminder that EVERY minority group is entitled to the respect of a moment or two's thought. Shouldn't we all be seeking to ensure that every member of society gets a square deal?

WEEK 7

Our tribal memory

Historical work which I have done has enriched my *memory* of things past. Family history has carried me back firmly for five hundred years and in a stuttering way several centuries further. But what of my own memory?

Even that takes me back about one hundred and fifty years! How so? My grandparents were born in the 1860s and my parents in the 1890s. Through their genuine memories my *tribal memory* goes back long before my birth, and these older memories have affected my life. So it is with all of us.

My parents told me little bits about their parents and rather more about themselves as did my Auntie Gladys. So my first significant *memories* include such things as Queen Victoria's Diamond Jubilee and her funeral, and the Boer War!

But it was the First World War that dominated all memories when I was a child, surpassing even more recent events such as the General Strike of 1926 and the Great Depression which began in 1929. Even as a child I was conscious of the cloud the first war left hanging over us, a cloud which became palpable as the Second World War approached. There were constant reminders of the first war in the men with war injuries, kerbside match sellers, disabled bands and straightforward beggars.

Strangely enough two elements of this were to come back to haunt me later in my life. In Bamber Bridge, Preston in the 1950s the cotton mills were closing down. There was a cloud of uncertainty over the future which governed all sorts of simple decisions in life. It was a cloud you could feel.

And in Derbyshire in the 1960s the same thing was happening with the coal mines - but there I was reminded of the First World War in another way. My first impression of Derbyshire was of the large number of injured men about - the result of mining injuries.

Of course, when I was at school several of my teachers had been in the First World War. One could still be disturbed by the noise and had something akin to fits when he would go almost berserk. One had been gassed and only had one lung. He always insisted on cleaning the blackboard himself to limit the dust that flew. And if you stood too close to him when your exercise book was being marked you could be sure of:

"Stand aside boy. Don't breathe your filthy breath down my clean neck!"

Another had fought at the Somme and survived. He never spoke of the war but he introduced us to poets like Wilfred Owen and he always ensured that Remembrance Day was observed with dignity and reverence.

Their feelings were perhaps summed up by George Vallins (one of my English teachers) in his book *Sincere Flattery: Parodies from Punch (1954)*. In a poem called *A Kentish Lad* written in June 1945 at the end of the Second World War he wrote:

"........ for these, their warfare over, the umpire calls in vain, batsman and slip and cover return not back again, who other fields defended, their silent watches keep, the lads who walk unfriended the joyless fields of sleep."

As well as the First World War, I have memories of the General Strike and the Great Depression, both of them from before my life-time. But then personal memories take over - over seventy years of them now. I began to write my memories down only to have one of them challenged and shown to be incorrect. I had made my class at school the heroes in an incident which belonged to another class entirely. Memory makes heroes of us all!

So I decided to fictionalise my early memories and they grew to become three books: *An Evacuee, A Prized Pupil and A Reluctant Seaman.*

Through other people's writings, and more recently through film, radio and television and, through our children, the tribal memories of the past influence each new generation. They also ensure that our little lives are much longer and much bigger than we ever realise.

Brian Patten wrote:

"How long does a man live after all?"

"A man lives for as long as we carry him inside us, for as long as we carry the harvest of his dreams, for as long as we ourselves live holding memories in common, a man lives."

WEEK 8

Tolerance

Christians set great store by words purporting to come
from Jesus where he says "I am the way, the truth and the
life." He goes on to make it quite clear that he believes that
there is no other way and no other truth. As a non-
Christian I find that incredibly arrogant.

Intolerance is often based on arrogance - the arrogance of
the closed mind; the arrogance of those who believe that
they know best; the arrogance of dogmatism. It is also often
based on insecurity and fear.

The dogmatist has a closed mind. It has a mind that has
often been donated to a particular ism. Once you have
given your mind away you have no further need of thought.
Others can think for you. All you have to do is *trust and
obey* as the old hymn puts it. Once the mind has been
donated, the dogmatist becomes imprisoned within his chosen system of thought and belief and he fears anything
which could damage or destroy the security that imprison-
ment gives.

Tolerance on the other hand, can be based on an incredibly
casual carelessness. This is the carelessness of those who
have no firm convictions of their own. They are happy for
anyone to believe anything they like just so long as they are
left in peace. This is not the kind of tolerance I wish to
advocate.

The tolerance I am interested in is a tolerance which com-
bines firm conviction with genuine humility. Intolerant people seek to impose their own beliefs and practices on every-
body else. Tolerant people recognise their own inadequacy
and extrapolate from that the claim that no one has the
right or the knowledge or the understanding to tell anyone
else how to think or how to live.

If no one has the right to tell others how to think and how to live it follows that I have no right to attempt these things. No human being can be *the way* for any other. We do not exist to play the game of *follow my leader*. Each of us has to make his or her own way through life and it is sheer presumption for anyone to try to tell us how.

Socrates claimed that the only thing he knew was that he knew nothing. Tolerant people begin where Socrates claimed to be. We begin in ignorance and no matter how much we learn along the way we only discover how little we know. This does not preclude firm convictions but it does mean that our convictions must be allied to an open mind, a readiness to learn and if need be, to change.

If we have an open mind then we recognise that no matter how firmly we believe what we do, we may be wrong. Bertrand Russell was asked if he would die for his beliefs. "Good heavens no!" he replied. "I might be wrong." An open mind is also based firmly on the recognition that we always have much to learn. And thirdly, an open mind is based on the conviction that there is nothing to fear in learning.

The intolerant are afraid or unable to risk opening their minds to new knowledge and new ideas. Tolerant people are open to such things. They recognise that there is plenty of room for alternative ideas and systems of thought to live side by side amicably. PROVIDED THEY DO NO HARM those alternatives must be free to exist.

But that proviso is an important one. There are limits to tolerance.

As an atheist I can live happily alongside Christians or Muslims or people of any other thought or belief system. But there are occasions where their teachings and their practice seem to me to become harmful and dangerous. At that point tolerance goes out of the window. Let me give two examples.

I am opposed to the state subsidising religious and all other private schools. There are two reasons for my opposition. The first is that private schools of any persuasion are socially divisive and the dangers of such divisiveness have been demonstrated very clearly in Northern Ireland. If people want private schools or religious schools, let them pay for them themselves 100%. If they had to, most would then disappear overnight.

The second example is this: I cannot tolerate a good deal of religious teaching on sex and sex related subjects. Their teaching and practice is often unnatural, harmful and downright dangerous. A study of behaviour of Catholic and Muslim authorities in Africa demonstrates very clearly the dangers of their teaching. By their opposition to the *safe sex* campaign they have actively contributed to the spread of Aids and hindered all attempts to halt its spread.

Their teaching and their behaviour are intolerable.

So there are limits to tolerance but most of us set those limits too tightly.

Tolerance involves taking risks. The only limit is the limit I have suggested: anything goes provided that it does no harm. That surely is the foundation of all morality and of all of life: to do all the good we can and as little harm.

Tolerance sets us free to accept and work with others in a non-judgemental way for the good of the whole community.

WEEK 9

An Abandoned Car

We first noticed it when we were about to have lunch. A red jaguar was parked in the middle of the field. It had smashed through the hedge up on the main road. As the crow flies it wasn't far away but we'd have to walk a good half mile to get to it.

"Kids!" I grumbled, "probably high on drugs or booze."

Wendy suggested that I should ring the police but I didn't want to get involved. It took her a while to persuade me to do my duty. The police asked if I knew the registration number. I didn't but I promised to walk over to the car and find out for them.

What didn't stike them and what didn't strike us until after I had rung the police, was this:

Suppose it was not kids (it wasn't). Suppose someone had fallen asleep at the wheel or had had a heart attack. Someone could still be in the car.

When I finally arrived at the car I was mightily relieved to find no one in it. But just imagine: my lack of interest, concern, curiosity and compassion could have meant the difference between life and death for someone. Sometimes we need to overcome our natural unwillingness to get involved.

WEEK 10

An Old Colliery

In Frank Palmer's book *Unfit To Plead* I read about an old colliery. It brought back memories of my only journey down the pit. A friend who was a mine manager arranged the trip and took me down. We were properly helmeted, kitted and knee padded.

I expected the cage to lurch downwards and to move at a speed beyond any lift I had ever experienced so it didn't bother me when it did. It was a long way down but that didn't bother me either. We came out of the cage into a well lit road in which we could walk side by side with plenty of space all around. It was fascinating and quite pleasant except that I was very soon aware of the constant creaking and groaning of the walls all around as they strove to demolish the structures protecting us and to collapse into the open space where we were.

As we drew nearer to the coal face I became aware of the noise of the trepanner cutting into the coal. It was a vast machine and deafening. But there were areas it couldn't reach where men still worked with picks cutting out the coal by hand. And the easy, pleasant walking was over now. The seam of coal was about 3'6" and that was the height in which men worked. They thought that that was pretty good. The older ones of them remembered days when they had to cut coal lying on their sides with a seam a little over 2' to cut out. In these softer days of the 1960s such seams were ignored and left unworked.

We had no sooner arrived than the machine stopped. The silence was eerie, awe inspiring, and I was conscious once more - only more strongly now - of the creaks and groans all around us.

When a coal face was almost exhausted, the road to it was carefully maintained but the exit road was allowed to collapse. At the coal face I visited, all that was left of the exit road was a narrow tunnel carrying a moving belt on which the cut coal was loaded. The miners leaving work lay on the belt and were carried back to the cage.

My friend used the silence to show me the coal face and to tell me about the work done there and then we went to follow the miners out on the moving belt. But before long, the belt stopped!

I have always suspected that I owed this to my friend. I think he kept me there deliberately so that the belt would stop when we were in the tunnel. Why take me that way anyhow? We could perfectly easily have walked back the way we came. But none of these things struck me at the time. All I knew was that we were in this narrow tunnel with no means of going back. So we crawled on our bellies until we arrived at the cage at last.

Funnily enough, I was concentrating so hard on crawling that I felt no fear until afterwards. Fear is a funny thing. I can break out into a sweat now sometimes when I think of that journey half a mile or more underground. I certainly never wanted to go down a pit again.

To visit a pit like that is one thing. WORKING down there with the constant knowledge in the back of your mind that there were dangers of rock falls, of flooding, or of an explosion of gas, cannot be imagined.

The destruction of the mining industry under Margaret Thatcher was done badly, brutally and callously with no regard for the pit communities and no proper support for families whose menfolk were thrown out of work. But thinking miners never wanted their sons to follow them down the pit and we should be thankful that few in this country now work in those dreadful conditions.

WEEK 11

The Homeless

In his "Biography Of London" Peter Ackroyd has a vivid description of London at night. Over a period of twenty years I often found myself in London at night with time to kill. Goodness knows how many hours I have spent wandering the streets there.

When I was a young man many of the West End streets were unpleasant to walk because there were prostitutes every few yards touting for business. There were still a few about but in my time most of them relied on the telephone and the kiosks were full of their cards. I wonder whether mobile phones have put an end to this kind of advertising?

My own walks in London were mostly a pretty dull passing of the time, looking at shop windows full of things I would never want to buy. Some areas were packed with people although even those thinned out in the early hours of the morning. But mostly, London was dull, empty and safe.

Near Charing Cross, in the gardens, I once met a group of men I had known when I worked at Botleys Park Hospital which was once a large hospital in Chertsey - a hospital for mentally handicapped people. I worked there for four years.

Now these men were enjoying a change in government health care policy. They were now freed from life in the safe confines of a large institution and living in the community. But whatever provision had been made for them was clearly not working. They had simply become additions to London's huge population of vagrants.

I remember once being in Victoria Station when its resident population of vagrants moved out for the night. Warned by messages over the tannoy they emerged from all over the station - behind advertising hoardings, from building sites, from stairways, porches, all manner of holes and corners, any place that gave them a hidey hole. It reminded me of nothing so much as cockroaches in a naval kitchen where I once did seven weeks *work ship.*

It was an incredible and distressing sight. In wealthy England this was what so many of my fellow human beings had come to.

WEEK 12

Marriage

From time to time I am invited to conduct an illegal marriage ceremony.

Perhaps I had better rephrase that. There is nothing illegal about it but there is nothing legal either. It is a marriage ceremony without any legal standing because the Government still won't allow humanist celebrants to act as nonconformist ministers often do, conducting ceremonies with the registrar present to register the marriage.

The marriages I conduct usually follow several meetings with the couple, meetings where we work out exactly what they want their marriage ceremony to say. At the first meeting they usually don't know so I give them a specimen ceremony which is fairly traditional in style. Part of that specimen contains a passage which talks about the ideal and purpose of marriage.

I was brought up within the Christian tradition where the ideal couples aimed at was that of a marriage of one man and one woman joined for life. Even though I have failed to live up to that tradition myself, I felt it was a pretty good ideal to aim at. But I have found over the years that that is the one part of my specimen ceremony that nearly all couples tear up and re-write! Most non-religious young people today seem unwilling to commit themselves to a life-long union of complete faithfulness.

Why should they? Why should we expect it of them when so many of us have failed to keep the vows we made - and that includes many who have stayed together. We need the honesty to admit that people make mistakes and also that people change, and when they do, they do not do so in tandem.

36

And why should the churches make such a meal of this? They aren't ALL rigid but many of them are reduced to pathetic hypocrisy. I was asked to marry a Roman Catholic girl whose marriage had broken down and who was divorced. She had gone to her Priest and asked him to marry her. He said,
"If you can tell me that your marriage was never consummated I will marry you."

"But I can't do that. You know me and you know my children. How could I say such a thing?"

She was so disgusted that she came to see me. Even when the church is not as bad as that, it is often pretty awful. Think of the second marriage of Prince Charles. He could not marry in church because the church does not recognise divorce or allow those who have been divorced to re-marry. Strictly speaking that means that marriages of divorced people in a registry office are not marriages at all in the sight of God.

So according to their God, divorced people are still married. People re-married in a registry office are not married in the sight of God. (Some would say that no one married in a registry office is married in the sight of God.) Yet - and this seems to me to be the church's supreme hypocrisy:

People can still go from the registry office to the church and God will bless their non-marriage!

Historically, in different parts of the world, a host of different kinds of relationship has been acceptable and often the norm. This includes both multiple relationships - a man with many wives or a woman with many husbands - and the single-sex relationships that tend to dominate today's newspapers.

Why should we not be flexible enough to acknowledge the widest variety of human relationships? Whether we call them marriages or not is irrelevant nor should the law concern itself with them. As long as relationships are freely entered into; as long as those who have entered into relationships are protected; and as long as any children are protected too and their rights secured; people should be free to live in whatever way they choose. The only place for the law is in securing those rights and in ensuring that when relationships break down, all those affected should have the equal protection of the law and the same rights in law.

WEEK 13

Amoral Animals

We are animals. We may not like to be reminded of the fact but that is what we are. We share 98.5% of our genes with the chimpanzees. We are animals. That is one of the supreme facts about us.

Like other animals we were conceived and born. We live and we shall die. We had a beginning and we shall have an end. It is as simple as that. We are just animals. And we have precisely the same primary concerns as the rest of the animals. When life is at its lowest ebb or at its most basic there are only three things that matter, food, shelter and reproduction.

All animals spend their lives finding food, finding or making some sort of shelter from the elements, and mating in order to perpetuate their own kind. Some of them are faithful to one partner. Many of them are not. Some of them bring up their children until they are independent. Others leave the job to their partners in sex or even, like cuckoos, to chosen nurses.

Humans are animals. Masses of them live lives so basic that those three primary concerns take up virtually the whole of their lives. For the rest of us the quest for food and shelter has become incredibly complex. We do all sorts of things that seem to have nothing to do with food and yet, in the end, everything we do has to do with food. Whether we work as mechanics or miners or in the media we are all working to earn our daily bread. That is what work is all about. And we are working to earn enough to pay the rent or mortgage to provide a home or shelter from the elements.

Those of us who have risen above the basic struggle for life make more and more demands. We are not satisfied with the kind of shelter our parents strove for. We tend to want to start our lives where they left off. Their dreams become our basics. For my generation washing machines, fridge-freezers, dish-washers, television and central heating were all luxuries. Now couples expect to begin their lives together with all of these things.

Strip us off though. Peel away the layers we have added. What is left? We may not like the title but we are animals. There is no mystique and no supernatural. We are animals just like other animals.

And at that basic level there is no morality either. Morality is a luxury superimposed on life when we rise above the basics. But strip us down to our essentials and morality goes out of the window. We will do anything to survive. We will lie, cheat, beg, borrow or steal. We will do whatever we have to do to ensure that we have food and shelter. We will do whatever it takes to look after number one, and perhaps number two, three and four! As Gary Kasparov put it: "When survival is at stake, there is no room for morality." That may sound terrible but it happens to be the simple truth. Study anyone who has been reduced to rock bottom and see how he climbs out of the pit. The world does not owe us a living and basically doesn't give a damn if we are without a living. If we are not prepared to fight for ourselves and for our own survival, no one else will. And fighting for survival can be a desperate business in which there are no rules. Whatever we have to do we will do. Humans learned that very early in their history. They learned to stand on their own two feet and when we are desperate enough, we learn to do the same.

WEEK 14

Morality and Ethics

Can you remember what I had to say about human beings at their most desperate. I claimed that they would do ANYTHING to survive. Law and morality had no meaning for them at all.

Victor Hugo's *Les Miserables* depicts a man who steals bread so that his family may eat. The only people who care about stealing are the people who have things worth stealing.

We are often told that humans have devised laws and moral codes for the protection of the weak. It isn't true. Laws and moral codes are for the protection of the rich against the desperate. Francis Bacon quotes a saying that laws are like cobwebs where the weak are caught and the strong break through.

Morality is a luxury! That doesn't mean that it isn't important. But it's not until we have risen above mere survival that we can begin to think about things like the right way to live or about goodness and virtue. For human animals survival always comes first. Only those whose lives are secure can bother about morality. It is no accident that the clergy are one of the groups who have concentrated on morality most. Their lives are secure. Their income is secure. Provided they live within it, they have no financial or material worries at all.

For most of the rest of us life is a struggle and morality a luxury. I preached once at a service organised by a Rotary group. Afterwards one business man said to me, "You ask too much." Now that I have spent a large part of my life trying to survive as a businessman I think he was probably right. I have also come to the very firm conclusion that a great deal of the morality of groups like the clergy is mistaken. Sometimes, as I have already mentioned, it is so wrong that it is dangerous and harmful to humanity. The spread of Aids owes more than a little to the moral attitudes of both Roman Catholicism and Islam.

As an atheist do I have any moral viewpoint at all then? Or, are Christians right when they denounce atheists as immoral? Certainly it is true that an atheist has no morality imposed from above. Our morality is chosen and thought out by ourselves. So it is not something fixed. It is always developing and there is always fine tuning going on.

When I was at university I studied ethics as one of my intermediate courses. I remember virtually nothing of the course except the opening definition in a very opaque textbook: "Ethics is the study of what is right and good in conduct." Recently I have read an A Level course book called *Science In Society*. It may come as a surprise to find me reading a book about science for I am the greatest scientific ignoramus in the world. But one of my daughters wrote part of the book so I had to read it! In it she defines ethics as *the branch of philosophy concerned with how we should decide what is morally wrong and what is morally right.* And she goes on to suggest four *widely used ethical frameworks* which help us to decide *whether something is ethically acceptable or not.*

No one of them is adequate on its own. The four have to be taken together and balanced against one another before we can come to responsible ethical decisions. The first of them involves a balancing of rights. Individual rights have to be balanced against the rights of society as a whole; local rights against national; national against international. I mentioned Victor Hugo's *Les Miserables* which asks us to balance the right of a poverty stricken family to life against the rights of property and the laws against stealing.

The second is the utilitarian framework. When faced with ethical dilemmas utilitarians argue that the right decision *is the one that leads to the greatest good for the largest number of people.* So we have to look at the possible or probable consequences of our actions and seek to act in ways that bring the greatest benefits to the environment, to other people and to ourselves.

Third: the study of ethics requires us to act as adults, to think for ourselves, and to make our own *informed decisions and then to put them into effect.* But if they are to be informed decisions, then we must refer and sometimes defer to the thinking of others who have faced similar problems. We are not islands. We are interdependent beings and must always take into account the fact that our decisions will impinge on the lives of others.

The fourth framework my daughter mentions is that of justice, equality and fair play. Ethical decisions must always seek to ensure *fair treatment and the fair distribution of resources or opportunities.*

As I read my daughter's work I was impressed by the clarity and simplicity with which she expressed things which had seemed so complex and difficult when I was a student. The four frameworks within which she suggested that we work combine to make a very useful whole. But what also struck me was the fact that in all of this there are no figures of authority whether human or divine.

Society may have been simpler when other people told us what to do and we (sometimes) obeyed. But it is so much more satisfying when we are treated as adults and expected to live and think as adults. The study of ethical questions is a rational exercise of human minds. It is our attempt to come to an agreed way through complex and difficult issues. As we think and puzzle together we find our own answers to difficult questions and in doing so we establish our own morality for today, and as a foundation from which our children can move forward.

WEEK 15

Personal Responsibility

In a local Church Of England newsletter I read: "At birth
we inherit a fallen nature, due to the disobedience of Adam
and Eve and we also inherited an inclination to selfishness
and sin."

I was astonished. It is over fifty years since I became a minister of religion (and over thirty since I left!) As far back as
that I felt that this kind of teaching was all behind us as
Christians. Surely nobody in their right mind believed it
any more!

Yet here was a priest writing of Adam and Eve as if they
were real people and still teaching traditional, orthodox
Christian doctrine that from conception we are all sinners
in need of salvation due to the disobedience of Adam and
Eve. This doctrine of original sin claims that we have all
inherited infection from their sin. And what was their sin
(apart from the sin of disobedience to God's authority)? It
was the sin of hunger for knowledge! There always have
been those in religion who have felt that knowledge was
dangerous. That is the underlying reason that Taliban
extremists burn girls schools and try to keep girls away
from schools. Imagine what a dreadful thing it would be if
girls began to think for themselves and even outdo boys!
But I digress.

There are many Christians who, unlike our priest, do not
believe in Adam and Eve. And many of them do not believe
in the doctrine of original sin either. Such Christians share
the view that I have always held that we come into this
world with a clean sheet and proceed to cover it with our
own unique handwriting, some of it good and some of it
bad; some of it positive and some of it negative.

How far we are free to choose between good and bad is a matter of endless debate. There can be no doubt that our area of choice is pretty limited. But my own view has always been that we have enough freedom to leave us responsible for the choices we make.

If we set to one side (for a few weeks) the choices we make in the heat of passion:

There are choices we make after long consideration of all the options, and there are choices we make on the hoof. Most of these choices will be the expression of the ideals upon which we seek to base our lives.

It seems to me to be important to have ideals - targets which we aim for and never fully achieve. My own comes from the line of a hymn: *To be the best that I can be.*

But it is the best that I can be. Not the best that you can be. You may be a brilliant artist, sculptor, carpenter, builder, mechanic - a host of things I could never aspire to be. I have no gifts in those directions. As individuals we are all different, with different capacities, different qualities and different talents. There is no need for any of us to try to be anything other than what we are. Our goal should be simply to be the best we, as individual persons can be. That is what the ancient Greeks meant when they urged us to seek excellence or virtue. Virtue is not a universal something for philosophers to try to define. Virtue is an individual thing - a making the most and making the best of what we have and are.

But the supreme danger in such a quest is the danger of a kind of cocky pride or arrogance. Such pride is very visible in ancient Athens and it was in evidence again in Renaissance Italy. So our quest for the best needs to be allied to Stoic self- restraint and modesty. And those should go together with two elements in the teaching of Epicurus, a teacher Christians maligned and deliberately misunderstood because he was in some respects so much in advance of their own teachings.

First, like the Stoics, he stood for simplicity in life. He believed that there are more important things than material possessions. He turned away from luxury (not least in food where he has been so completely misrepresented.) He believed that it really is true that *enough is as good as a feast.*

And second, Epicurus focussed on the fact that we are social animals. Central to life for the Epicurean is the concept of friendship. The Epicureans were the very first to teach that friendship knows no bounds. Friendship is not judgemental. It is not hampered or limited by such things as colour, sex, age or status. Friendship is open - open to all men, all women, all children - to all alike. It is one of the greatest secrets of true happiness.

So let us have no more of this stuff about original sin and the ideas of guilt, judgement, punishment in hell fire that go with it. Instead let us quietly acknowledge that we began as pure and innocent babies. We have had successes and failures since and some of us have blotted our copy-books badly. So we are all imperfect. But if we are genuinely trying to live our lives to the best of our ability; if we are trying to get on well with our neighbours in a spirit of friendship; if we are trying to be the best that we can be in our individual lives; then we can rest content.

If we are atheists we really can rest content with that. If we are religious we shall perhaps recognise that any god worthy of our worship would be more than content wi th such worshippers! There is no need for hair shirts or *wailing and gnashing of teeth.*

WEEK 16

The Imperfections Of Jesus

A friend of mine has asked me to write about the imperfections of Jesus, so here goes. I should begin with a caveat.
When I speak of Jesus I am referring to the picture we have
of him in the New Testament. After all there is no other.
But no one knows how accurate that picture is.

I was brought up to believe that Jesus is perfect - *is*
because through the resurrection he lives in the present.
Later my theological training underlined that; Jesus is perfect man and perfect God.

I still don't know why it took me so long to question that
teaching. It was a vicar's wife who enabled me to take the
first step. A group of us were discussing an incident in the
childhood of Jesus.

He and his parents had been to Jerusalem. When they set
off for home, Jesus remained behind, full of questions for
the priests in the Temple. At last his parents woke up to
the fact that he wasn't with them or their friends. In a
panic they hurried back to Jerusalem and searched for him
for days before finding him in the Temple.

He didn't apologise for staying without asking or telling
them. Boy-like, he was completely unaware of the agony
they had endured and only criticised them for not realising
where he would be.

The vicar's wife said, "If I had been his mother, I would
have given him a good hiding."

It was at this point that I realised that Jesus had all the
faults of any normal boy. He was fully human, and being
fully human, he was imperfect.

Little by little all sorts of other things caught my eye. There was the occasion when he was hungry and turned to a fig tree for figs. As a countryman he ought to have known full well that figs were out of season but he cursed the fig tree.

Another time a woman came to him for help when he was tired. He was just as grumpy as any of us would have been.

I also began to see that UNLESS THEY ARE TRUE, some of his claims are incredibly arrogant. I have mentioned elsewhere his words, "I am the way, the truth and the life. No one comes to the Father but by me." Not by Krishna or by the Buddha or Mohammed, or even Confucius or Epicurus, but *by me.* There is only one exclusive path and all other paths are damned. Only through Jesus and the salvation he achieves for us through his death can we find acceptance with God.

Those claims are breath-taking in their arrogance and make a complete mockery of inter-faith dialogue.

I think it was the salvation theology of the Christian Church and the *all the other paths are damned* bits of the teaching of Jesus which finally put me off him - and there are lots of them.

I listened to a clergyman taking a funeral and was astonished to hear him re-telling a story of Jesus about a wedding. Twelve girls had lanterns to light the way to the wedding but only six had enough forethought to take spare oil for their lamps. The others were far too excited to think about a thing like that - so their lamps ran out. The six who <u>were</u> prepared refilled their lamps but weren't prepared to risk helping the others. So the unprepared six went off to get some more oil and were late for the wedding. When they arrived THEY WERE NOT ALLOWED IN.

Would any ordinary, decent family have excluded them? Yet the all-loving God will have nothing to do with them!

48

The same is true of another story where someone turns up for a feast in the wrong clothes.

And Jesus tells stories of people separated like sheep and goats - sheep to heaven and goats to exclusion. Quite apart from the injustice to goats......

There is so much judgmental stuff in the New Testament that I find repulsive.

There is of course, another side to the coin. Jesus did many lovely things and told many lovely stories as a part of his teaching. Stories like the Good Samaritan and the Prodigal Son deserve to live forever. Just because Jesus was imperfect (*was* because the resurrection is a myth) is no reason to reject him totally.

But it is a reason to reject Christian theology totally. The imperfections of Jesus and of his teachings demonstrate how truly human he was and that talk of his divinity is rubbish. We are all imperfect, but perhaps there are elements in all of our lives which are worthy of praise. If we bother to look at Jesus or at the New Testament it IS worth looking for those elements.

WEEK 17

Salvation

The idea of salvation from sin to a new life of holiness, purity and virtue is central to the Christian faith. This salvation is achieved for us by Jesus and supremely by his sacrificial death upon the cross. His is the perfect sacrifice, not least because he alone is a perfect and sinless man.

I have already shown that from the testimony of the New Testament alone, no matter what his quality, it simply is not true that Jesus was perfect. He had all the faults and frailties of any other decent human being.

But we'll play 'let's pretend' for a while. Let's pretend that Christian claims are true and that Jesus was the perfect sacrifice. That raises more questions than it answers and Christians themselves wrestle with some of them. Two obvious ones are: to whom is the sacrifice made? And if the answer to that is God, what sort of a God is it who requires human sacrifice of this kind? Let's not go beyond that to the incredibly complex question of how Jesus can be divine, one with the Father, the recipient of this sacrifice, and yet at the same time be the human sacrifice.

Instead let us ask the simpler question: HOW does the sacrifice of Jesus save people from their sins?Some Christians say that Jesus was the perfect moral example to us, inspiring us to follow him. But that doesn't require sacrificial death. It ducks the question of his death on the cross, seen as a voluntary sacrifice chosen by Jesus himself. His blood is *the blood of the Lamb* shed for us and somehow purifying us. How?

Christians speak of his death as a vicarious sacrifice, or (as Paul put it) as paying the price of our sin, our ransom from the slavery of sin to enable us to enter into the freedom of the children of God.

But that question 'how' remains. How does HIS death deal with MY sin??

In the end, NONE of the Christian answers deals with that question. And the reason is very simple. NO ONE, neither Jesus nor any other religious leader can deal with any sin other than his own, NO ONE. It is as I ask my next question that that will become clear.

The Christian doctrine of salvation begins with the assumption that we are all sinners in need of salvation because imperfect beings cannot enter into the kingdom or the presence of God. Methodists used to recite, almost as a mantra,

"All men need to be saved; all men can be saved; all men can be saved to the uttermost."

But is it true that all men (and women too) need to be saved?

I've no doubt that most of us would admit that we could be better than we are. But my impression after visiting say 15 to 20 thousand homes over the course of the last 60 years is that most of us are pretty decent, honourable people. I would go further and say that most of us are perfectly fit and worthy to enter into the presence of any of the gods I have ever heard of. After all, according to religion, they made us the kind of creatures we are in the first place.

And even those few who do need saving, very rarely need to be saved from SIN. There may be one or two people who are incorrigibly and fundamentally bad and who, if there were a god would need to be saved from his wrath but I've yet to meet one. Oh, I've met some pretty horrible people in my time, people I never want to meet again, but I've never met anyone I would consign to hellfire. Have you?

The people I have met who actually need to be saved are not people in the grip of sin. They are those who have been overwhelmed by their passions and they are those who are in the grip of an addiction.

All our talk of ethics and morality has assumed that we are rational beings who think out our path before taking action. The truth is that we are also people of passion and sometimes our passions are so powerful that they can take control of our lives completely. Passion can override all our careful thinking and all our intentions whether good or bad. Passion can lead to the most precious and wonderful moments of our lives and can be the beginning of a whole lifetime of good things. But it can also be disastrous and destructive.

I have known men with diabolical tempers who have done a great deal of harm to those who were closest to them. The harm cannot be undone, but some of those men, by the force of their own determination and will power, learned to bring their tempers under control.

The power of sexual passion is another that can be overwhelming for good or for ill. The apostle Paul reckoned that if sex is your passion you had better get married! But marriage is not necessarily the answer. It can even exacerbate the problem.

The real answer is to find someone whose sexual drive matches your own, someone who can share your passion to the full. In such partnerships the power of sex is harnessed and brought within bounds to the enrichment of both partners. It becomes the power which drives the relationship, something very wonderful, beautiful, fulfilling and terrific fun.

Addiction is a different matter altogether and perhaps we had better leave that for another week.

WEEK 18

Tragedy and Triumph

Every so often I find myself conducting the funeral of someone who has died as a result of drug or alcohol addiction.
They are usually well attended and many in the congrega-
tions are themselves in the grip of these addictions. I
always try to say something that may prove to be the spark
that leads someone to take the first steps back and I
always come away feeling disheartened and useless.

There have been times when my life has brought me into
much closer contact with addicts. There was a time when
professionals sent people on to me. Having failed to achieve
anything themselves, they seemed to think that there was a
chance that I might succeed where they had failed. I'm not
aware that I ever did. It was utterly depressing and yet we
went on hoping against hope.

Addictions are illnesses and need to be understood in that
light. But they are illnesses which often undermine and
destroy personal relationships leaving trails of unhappiness
and often guilt. Yet I never cease to be amazed at the
understanding and kindness shown by many family members and friends.

Such people have learned to focus on the fact that addiction is illness, not sin or wickedness. So, when we are
thinking about addicts, that is the first thing that needs to
be said about them. It is no use standing in judgement
over an addict. Addicts do need saving but who can save
them? At the most fundamental level, at the deepest and
most truthful level of all, the answer is NO ONE - no one,
that is except themselves.

That is not to say that no one can help. Those who need to
be saved from addiction will certainly need all the help that

is available. But all the help in the world will not save them unless they themselves take the first step, and that is the loneliest and hardest step of all. Until you have actually put your foot on the first rung of the ladder, there is no hand that can actually reach far enough to help you.

What is more, at every other rung of the ladder it is all too easy to fall back and none of those helping hands can prevent the fall. So ultimately, EVERY step is a step you have to take yourself.

I know these things both from what I have seen, and also because, in a rather different way, I have been there.

If any of us need to be saved it is no use turning to Jesus or to anyone else. We have to save ourselves. The only thing I would add to that is my simple conviction that although comparatively few do, ANYONE CAN. I know this because just occasionally I come across someone who has bucked the norm. It takes honesty and humility to acknowledge that there is a problem and to accept all the help that is available. And then it takes incredible qualities of character: courage, determination, consistency and staying power.

Rehabilitation and recovery are all too rare, but there are people who achieve these things. One such person was a man who not only bucked the trend but went straight back to the places where he was most in danger. He had been in the grip of alcoholism but went straight back to the pubs to join his friends enjoying pub quizzes. He had to remain completely (and I mean completely) teetotal.

Somehow he managed to achieve just that, and after training with the people who had helped him achieve his own success, he spent the rest of his life working with addicts and helping them to turn their own lives around. Cancer took Alan from us, but because of his life and achievements there are people still living who owe their lives to him.

Some of the most moving words in the story of the Prodigal Son are the words, "He was lost and is found." Alan was lost. Thanks primarily to his quality as a man, but also to his many helpers, he was found again. But he went much further than anything in the story of the Prodigal Son, for he became a part of the path of recovery for many others who were also lost and now are found.

WEEK 19

"Thou Shalt Not Judge"

We are all inclined to. Oh yes we are! We are all inclined to pass judgement on other people. We are all too quick and hasty in judgement.

I read recently of an old man whose grandson died when he was seven years old. The two had been very close. It was the grandfather who took the boy to and from school. It was the grandfather who took the boy to the park to play on the swings and roundabouts. And now the boy was dead.

In his grief, the grandfather took to going to the school to watch the other children at their play and at their sports. And he took to going to the park too. You can imagine that it wasn't long before the whispers began.

"It's that man again." "Do you notice, it's always the boys he watches, never the girls." And so on.......

When he died and stopped going to the school and the park, parents who knew nothing about him were relieved.

I've been fairly critical of Jesus in recent weeks, so let me point to the opposite side of the coin by mentioning a story about him which only got into the New Testament by the skin of its teeth - it was no part of the original four gospels but someone inserted it.

It tells the story of a woman who had been caught out committing adultery. (No one seems to have had any interest in the man involved.) The legal punishment was death by stoning!

As Jesus was in the area the authorities brought the woman to him and asked him what he thought they should do with her. Jesus looked at them and said,

"Let him who is without sin among you be the first to throw a stone at her."

Then he left them to it but of course he caught them out. The story continues: "When they heard it, they went away, one by one, beginning with the eldest, and Jesus was left alone with the woman standing before him. Jesus looked up and said to her,

Has no one condemned you?... Neither do I condemn you; go, and do not sin again.' (John chapter 8).

Notice that Jesus said, "Neither do I condemn you." I find that particularly interesting because apparently the woman WAS guilty as charged. *She was caught in the very act. So why did Jesus not condemn her?*

Was he simply saying that he didn't think that the punishment fitted the crime? Or was he saying that even though she was guilty, she should not be condemned? Did he know something about her that we do not know?

Or even more radical than that, was he saying that adultery itself should not be condemned? Somehow I doubt if he would go quite that far. But perhaps in his treatment of this particular woman he was saying, *adultery should not ALWAYS be condemned.* Now that really would be something.

We don't know the answers to these questions but perhaps they are questions that need to be asked of us in our own human relationships and with our own human frailties.

The central message of the story is transparently clear. It is that none of us is so perfect that s/he can stand in judgement over someone else.

I would want to add one thing more. Very often when people pass judgement on their fellows, they do so without any first hand knowledge at all. They judge on the basis of any old gossip, tittle-tattle and rumour. They do so on the basis of stories that have been blown up out of all proportion; mountains that have been concocted from molehills or even from nothing at all.

It would make so much difference to human life and society if we all learned that we have no right and no competence to judge anyone except ourselves.

WEEK 20

Innocence

In his autobiography Richard Adams, the author of
Watership Down, recounts a childhood occasion when he
was out walking on his own. He came upon a man who had
made a small fire of sticks by a hedge. The man was brew-
ing up a mug of tea in a can.

He chatted with the eight year old boy and shared his mug
of tea with him and then they parted, never to meet again.

It reminded me of a story from East Anglia which I read
many years ago. A young girl told her mother about an old
man who was working on the road near their house. Her
mother sent her out with a mug of tea for him and over the
period of time he was working there, she got to know a
good deal about him.

He was in his eighties and lived in the local workhouse. For
the privilege of a roof over his head he was expected to
work - at this time as a stone breaker for the road
menders.

The mother in East Anglia had no hesitation in sending her
daughter out to the man and seems to have been quite
content that her young daughter should stay out there
chatting with the old chap.

Richard Adams' mother seems to have been perfectly at
ease with the idea of her son wandering alone in the countryside. The same was true of my own childhood.

After breakfast we all had our jobs to do. Once they were
done we were bundled out of the house, out of the way
while the real work was done. In suburbia we lived almost
opposite a park and spent most of our time there but from

the beginning of the Second World War I lived as an evacuee, first by the sea and then in a small country town, and after the war my parents moved into the country.

None of the people I lived with ever knew where I was, and when we moved back home my mother certainly didn't. But I can't imagine that any of them ever worried about where I was either - until I started staying out way beyond my bedtime.

Nowadays parents do worry. It must be extraordinarily difficult for children to enjoy the innocence of childhood as we did. Is the world really a much more dangerous place? For twenty years because of my work I roamed the streets of London alone at night and I never felt threatened. Is it just our media-fed perception of the world that makes it seem so dangerous?

I gave up reading a newspaper many years ago and now I've given up watching the news too (it's far too depressing.) Am I just putting my head in the sand or have I discovered something of the secret of childhood innocence once more?

WEEK 21

Toil and Leisure;
Work and Pleasure

On my birthday, I was talking on the phone to my daughter
Jean. She asked how I was going to spend the evening.

"I shall have a bath, tinkle on the piano and do a bit of
reading," I said.

She felt that retirement had a great deal to be said for it.
So it does. Yet there are times when retirement can leave
one feeling thoroughly useless and discontented. Nobody
needs us anymore.

The day after I spoke to Jean I found myself reading
Samuel Daniels' delightful poem "Ulysses and the Siren" in
an old 'Oxford Book of English Verse.' (How many children
or adults know Homer's stories nowadays I wonder?) In the
poem the Siren begins:

Come worthy Greek! Ulysses, come,
Possess these shores with me:
The winds and the seas are troublesome,
And here we may be free.
Here may we sit and view their toil
That travail on the deep,
And joy the day in mirth the while,
And spend the night in sleep.

But Ulysses is only interested in fame and honour:

...manliness would scorn to wear
The time in idle sport:
For toil doth give a better touch

To make us feel our joy,
And ease finds tediousness as much
As labour yields annoy.

The Siren suggests that Ulysses' toil is aimed at achieving a pleasure which, she claims, would be much more easily achieved with her. And then she says:

And ease may have variety
As well as action may.

It seems to me that both Ulyssess and the Siren are right!

Perhaps the secret of retirement is to find the Siren's secret: *Ease may have variety*. But we also need to recognise that ease can find *tediousness* unless we have enough useful labour to avoid it.

WEEK 22

The Limits Of Tolerance

When we work out our own philosophy of life, it is not long before we find that many other people have a similar philosophy. Nor will it be long before we discover that there are those who have very different ideas, ideas that may lead us into severe disagreements.

At times we may hate someone else's approach to life so much that we try very hard to persuade them to change. But if we end up on opposite sides of the fence it is important to acknowledge that each of us has the right to do so.

Each of us may think the other wrong. We may even think each other stupid! But ultimately we must recognise one another's right to think our own thoughts, to come to our own conclusions and to live and do as we think best. There comes a point where each of us stands where Martin Luther stood and says, "Here I stand. I can do no other."

Are there no limits to the tolerance this individual approach to philosophy demands?

We cannot limit or govern the way people think. But where their thinking is dangerous to other people and where it leads to anti-social behaviour, there society has the right to step in to limit or govern the expression of their thought in action.

Where our ideas are the same or similar, we shall be able to work together for the common good. It is vitally important that we should do so, that we should concentrate on our areas of agreement and work together wherever we can. Where our ideas are different let us debate or argue hammer and tongs, but always if we can in a spirit of friendship. And if we cannot find agreement, then let us *agree to differ,* going our own ways in a spirit of mutual respect.

Sometimes of course, even that is not possible. Sometimes we find that we have actively to oppose one another, perhaps to alter something in society that seems wrong to us but right to someone else. As I write, one issue in the news is the question of our right to choose to die and to be assisted when we do so. I am convinced that we should have this right. You may disagree. Does that mean that we can no longer be friends? Of course not.

It is almost always possible to strive might and main for our own ideas against other people and still to remain friends. The old tradition in the House Of Commons of meeting your enemy for a drink after fighting tooth and nail in the house is probably less common than one would wish, but it is a good tradition nonetheless.

Disagreements can stretch friendship to the limit but they should not be allowed to break it. If we have the humility to accept that we can always be wrong and if we live our lives in genuine mutual respect, friendship can almost always prove stronger than disagreement.

WEEK 23

Resignation and Acceptance

A friend wrote to me about the importance of always striving for the best solution to life's problems. She complained that *the older generation often* seem *resigned to life's difficulties.*

'Resignation' often used to be written about as if it were a virtue. I have never thought that it was. To be resigned to life's difficulties is to believe that we can do nothing about them. If we once believe that we are lost. My correspondent was right. We should never cease to strive to find the answer to life's problems and our own best way through and past them.

But striving is often very stressful both for those who are doing the striving and for those all around them. It is often a vain attempt to become something other than we are - something we do not have it in ourselves to be. It is often to be seen in religious people striving after an impossible perfection. You can see it in John Wesley before his conversion experience.

Somewhere along the line we need to come to some sort of acceptance of ourselves. For those of us who think hard and carefully about life and how we should live it, there comes a time when many of us feel that *we have gone about as far as we can go.*

That doesn't mean that we become complacent or that we close our minds and hearts to new ideas or passions. It does mean that we have found a philosophy of life which satisfies us and we have found a way of life that satisfies us too.

We can accept ourselves as we are in the knowledge that we shall usually aim for the best and highest we know without having to stop and think about it. That kind of acceptance takes much of the stress and striving out of life and leads to serenity.

I suspect that serenity and peace often seem boring qualities to the young. But as we grow older, many of us (not all of us) desire these qualities above almost all else. In so far as we find them we can rest content.

This is not resignation, nor is it laziness. It is the joy which comes from arriving at a satisfactory destination.

I suppose one day I shall talk to my correspondent about the fact that arrival at a destination is not an end so much as a new beginning!

WEEK 24

Romance

"He is in love with an ideal;
A creature of his own imagination;
A child of air; an echo of his heart;
And, like a lily on a river floating,
She floats upon the river of his thoughts."

Longfellow; the Spanish Student.

For centuries Europe's poets were in the grip of a romantic ideal of women and of courtship which bore little relation to the realities either of womanhood or of the marriage market. But the romantic ideal lived on.

Without putting it in to so many words, my father saw himself as a kind of knight in shining armour and a host of women as damsels in distress. Naive and foolish though it was, in him it was also an attractive fault which did no one any harm and which enabled him to be of genuine help to a lot of people in genuine need of help.

Unfortunately I grew up with much the same foolish idea both of women and myself.

Since the days of feminism and the emancipation of (European) women, I shouldn't think that many boys grow up with that kind of dream-world idea any more. That is mostly all to the good, but not entirely so.

The old ideals did mean that a man infected with them would treat a women with respect, courtesy and appreciation. It also meant that life could be full of romance and poetry. It was never reduced to physical need and biological necessity. Although all too often it focussed upon physical beauty, it was also an ideal which could focus on qualities of character and personality.

I suspect that this is one thing which has not changed. Young men still focus on physical beauty and young women, battered as they are by a host of advertisements, models and look-good articles in magazines, still worry far too much about how they look.

Perhaps it is only as we grow older that most of us learn to look beyond the surface and to see that true beauty depends on qualities of character rather than on skin texture and shape. As people grow older, it is their character and personality which shines through and as physical beauty fades, these are the things that make us feel that someone may be worth knowing.

We need today's earthy, hard-headed realism in our dealings with one another so that when we enter into deep relationships they are genuine. We need to love real people rather than *creatures of our imagination* otherwise our love will founder.

But this does not mean that there is no room for poetry in our relationships. Poetry and romance enrich relationships and carry them beyond the limited boundaries of ordinary life.

(And before you hasten to tell me, I do know that Longfellow was an <u>American</u> poet!)

WEEK 25

Spiritual

I think it would be true to say that I never use the word *spiritual*. This is a conscious and deliberate choice. There is always a better and more accurate word to describe what I want to say.

The word *spiritual* seems to be one of those vague, woolly words which people use to describe a host of different things, often with the implication of a hint of religiosity. When I sit down with families to prepare a funeral I'm often told,

"S/he wasn't at all religious but s/he was deeply spiritual." Because this is a sensitive and difficult time for them, I don't challenge their statement but I do try to probe a little to discover more precisely what they mean. Usually they mean no more than that the person we are talking about was thoughtful, decent, honourable or that s/he was some- one who felt at home with the world of nature.

In a passage quoted by Marilyn Mason in the New Humanist, the Dalai Lama wrote:

I believe there is an important distinction to be made between religion and spirituality. Religion I take to be con- cerned with faith in the claims to salvation of one faith tradi- tion or another, an aspect of which is acceptance of some form of metaphysical or supernatural reality... Connected with this are religious teachings or dogma, rituals, prayer and so on.

Spirituality I take to be concerned with those qualities of the human spirit - such as love and compassion, patience, toler- ance, forgiveness, contentment, a sense of responsibility, a sense of harmony - which brings happiness to both self and

others... There is thus no reason why the individual should not develop them, even to a high degree, without recourse to any religious or metaphysical belief system.

He is right. But there is also no reason why the individual should not develop these things without ever thinking of himself or herself as spiritual and without ever using the word. As Marilyn Mason said in her article,

"Many people would not necessarily call those human qualities which contribute to the happiness of oneself and others *spiritual* and *spirituality.* These nebulous words almost always require to be explained if they are to communicate clearly. In most cases it would be better to abandon them altogether and use one of the many more precise alternatives: moral, psychological, emotional, inspiring, imaginative, beautiful, life-enhancing, joyful, thoughtful, reflective, abstract, mysterious, weird, exciting, awe-inspiring...."

When we know what people mean by their word *spiritual* one or more of these words will always define their meaning more accurately and clearly. However, a look at those words will show that when people call someone *spiritual* they are almost always intending to praise and to express something good, something of quality.

This means that though we may never use the word, we shall be concerned to encourage people to develop the virtues the word implies. I don't usually have much fellow feeling for Paul, the self styled Christian apostle, but occasionally he seems to get things just right. In his letter to the Philippians chapter 4, verse 8 he wrote:

"Whatever is true, whatever is honourable, whatever is just, whatever is pure, whatever is lovely, whatever is gracious, if there is any excellence, if there is anything worthy of praise, think about these things."

Nothing about spirituality; nothing about religion; nothing about God or the gods - that is a message I can embrace wholeheartedly. And what a transformation it would make to life if we made such things the basis of all our thinking and of all our conversation and then tried to follow them through in our daily lives.

WEEK 26

Vocation

When I was a minister of religion I had a great deal of respect and affection for many of my collegues but I was also disappointed in many of them. We began with such high hopes and ideals but even before we left theological college there were those who were already quite clearly beginning to look out for number one. So, when I read Louis Auchincloss in his book *False Gods* (Constable 1993), his words rang bells:

"Worst of all... was the dulling effect on my spirits of the attitude of my fellow priests. Few if any of those whom I encountered in my daily work appeared to have much concern with a god of love and mercy. They were dryly dogmatic, wholly absorbed in the outward religious observances of their flock and bristling with hostility to anything that was not Catholic. Indigence and misery in the world around them hardly mattered: so long as heaven was offered to those who observed the rules..."

I suspect that this problem is greater in the Catholic Church than in many of the others. But in all churches there are a large number of clergy and ministers who have lost their way and who spend their lives focussing on the wrong things. I saw a cartoon recently with two priests walking together, talking about what they saw as the horrible possibility of female bishops. All around them as they walked there were people sleeping rough, youngsters taking drugs, people the worse for wear through alcohol and others knifing one another. The two priests were so engrossed with their crucially important discussion that they were completely oblivious to all that was going on around them.

But for many of the priests and ministers, it is not just that they have lost their way and become side-tracked into trivialities. There are a large number of them who have lost both their sense of vocation and their faith. I once asked a clergyman why he had remained in the church when he no longer believed. His wife replied bluntly, "Because it pays his stipend."

Having left the church in my early forties and discovered how useless my qualifications were in the outside world, I can understand that. Loss of belief is rarely complete. It is easy enough to go through the motions and to be a decent pastor. It is easy to offer gentle, uplifting homilies encouraging virtue, and to conduct the sacraments with care and dignity without actually believing in them. It is easy to look after church property and genuinely to earn your stipend without holding onto a genuine sense of vocation. Anyone of virtue and compassion can be trained to do a good job as a clergyman, no matter how slight his hold on the fundamentals of the Christian faith.

But so far, all of this has had to do with a vocation to Christian ministry. The word has been so much asscociated with religion that there are some dictionaries which only use it in the narrowest possible way. Traditionally Christians did extend its use to Christians in the medical profession - doctors and nurses and so on - and on to teachers. But they looked no further. Vocation was limited to people serving in these three professions.

That seems to me to be wholly wrong. I'm even tempted to speak of a thief as someone who has a vocation for burglary but perhaps that is going a little too far!

However, it does seem to me that anybody who consciously sets out to make the best use of his or her gifts and to use them in the service of others, can be spoken of as having a vocation.

So a carpenter, a plumber, a mechanic or a builder, a shopkeeper or an innkeeper, or anybody else can just as truly be described as having a vocation as a priest.

For some people that will imply having a call from God, but most of us who think of our work in vocational terms have no need for a call from a god to set us on our way. We do it because this is what we want to do. This is the way we want to live our lives, using whatever gifts we have in the service of other people.

WEEK 27

Francis Of Assisi

As a young man I found Francis of Assisi a great inspiration. There are words attributed to him which have been used as a prayer and turned into a hymn. Although I no longer have any belief in gods or religion, some of his words are still very important to me:

"Let us be instruments of peace.
Where there is hatred, let us sow love;
Where there is injury, pardon;
Where there is discord, union;
Where there is despair, hope;
Where there is darkness, light;
Where there is sadness, joy."

When we were school children, many of us were set the task of learning passages of poetry off by heart and those who belonged to churches were set to learn such things as the ten commandments or the creeds or the answers to a catechism. I was never any good at learning things that way. I could recite a couple of lines that had grabbed me, but never a whole poem.

Yet words do enter into our sub-conscious minds, and that is especially true of words that we use over and over again. I remember reading of a clergyman who was in prison, in solitary confinement. I can't remember why and I can't remember anything about him, but I do remember how he kept himself sane and healthy. He walked up and down his tiny cell recapturing and reciting in his head the Christian liturgy he had used so often and passages from the bible and prayers that had meant a lot to him. He was amazed at how much he could remember.

I know that I could do the same, both with Christian material and with my own secular *liturgies* since, and with prayers, thoughts, meditations, poems from a host of different sources. The words are all there and I could recall masses of them.

Such words can be a source of great comfort, strength and inspiration in times of need. But in those times when we are fit and well and on top of life, words are not enough. They have to be turned into the basis of our actions, and that is where good words from any source have their value. There aren't many better words than the ones with which I began this week's scribble.

WEEK 28

To Be Or Not To Be

Yesterday I conducted the funeral of a man in his forties who hanged himself. In the days before the funeral I found myself thinking about Hamlet's soliloquy:

"To be or not to be - that is the question:-

Whether 'tis nobler in the mind to suffer
the slings and arrows of outrageous fortune,
or to take arms against a sea of troubles,
and by opposing end them? - To die - to sleep -
No more; and by a sleep to say we end
the heartache and the thousand natural shocks
that flesh is heir to - It is a consummation
devoutly to be wish'd. To die - to sleep:-"

As I grow older it seems to me that there will come a time when I shall wish for that consummation. Even now there are times when I feel that I have outlived any usefulness I may once have had. In those moments life seems pretty pointless.

Hamlet introduces doubts and questions:

"To sleep; perchance to dream; - ay, there's the rub;
for in that sleep of death what dreams may come,
when we have shuffled off this mortal coil,
must give us pause: there's the respect
that makes calamity of so long life;
for who would bear the whips and scorns of time,
the oppressor's wrong, the proud man's contumely,
the pangs of despis'd love, the law's delay,
the insolence of office, and the spurns
that patient merit of the unworthy takes,
when he himself might his quietus make

with a bare bodkin?" (needle) "who would fardels" (burdens) "bear,
to grunt and sweat under a weary life,
but that the dread of something after death, -
the undiscover'd country, from whose bourn
no traveller returns, - puzzles the will,
and makes us rather bear those ills we have
than fly to others that we know not of?"

Nobody knows what lies after death. Different religions
have their hopes (and dreads) but no one <u>knows</u>.

My own view is quite clear. Together with all other living
things, I believe that when we die we die. That is it - end of
story.

We may call death a sleep, but people wake from sleep. I do
not believe that we wake from death. Nor do I believe that
we dream. I have no dread of anything *after death* for I
don't believe that there is anything after death.

The suicide chooses death because life seems unbearable.
The tragedy is that there is no going back on that choice,
and to loved ones it usually (not always) appears to be the
wrong choice. We make many wrong choices in life but suicide is the only one that is irreversible. And it leaves particular kinds of anguish behind: unanswered questions; feelings of guilt; frustration, bitterness and furious anger.

In brackets I included the words not always. I have known
suicides where people felt that the right choice had been
made and where they admired the courage involved in
making that choice.

It seems to me that suicide <u>always</u> demands courage. Just
as it takes courage to battle our way through *a sea of troubles*, so it takes courage to call a halt *and by opposing end
them* - to die.

In the past suicides were often condemned and their bodies were not allowed to lie alongside their *Christian* fellows. Imagine the pain and damage that caused their families and friends.

However wrong their choices may be, it is surely better to admire their defiance, their determination to hold their destiny in their own hands, their courage. And it is better too, to try to understand the desperation and depression that often drives them to their final choice.

Religion offers no comfort to those who mourn a suicide. The only thing that can bring a measure of comfort is a glimmer of understanding and a recognition of those qualities of character that enable someone to carry their choice through.

WEEK 29

Hell And Heaven

"Hell is one or our dogmas too you know."

"Yes, but... you don't have to believe anyone's in it."

"Hmm. I wonder. Would God have created something He had no use for? But certainly there's nothing that requires us to believe there are <u>many</u> people there. Perhaps only a tiny number."

... 'No, no, that would never do. If there were even one solitary soul languishing there, it would spoil heaven. For how could we go on forever and ever knowing that such suffering existed?...'"

Louis Auchinloss: False Gods - Constable 1993.

As a Christian I could never believe in hell because I never met anyone so evil that I would consign him to hell. And if I wouldn't, how could a loving God.

But what about heaven?

There are many people who have no formal religious belief but who cling on to some kind of belief in life after death together with the hope of reunion.

I'm normally confronted with such ideas just after someone has died, and that is no time to enter into a debate with people. Nor would I ever want to take away harmless ideas that people find helpful to them in times of need.

But their hopes have never really been thought through.

When you do begin to think them through, they raise a host of questions similar to the one raised in *False Gods.*

Assume for a moment that there is a life after death in some undefined *place.* It is a life without our earthly bodies. These have either been buried or burned. In the New Testament, Paul assumes that we shall have new, *spiritual bodies.* Will those new bodies somehow have continuity with the old so that we can recognise one another?

Will our future lives be the lives of bliss so many dream of? Whatever their dreams, they won't be the same as the old dreams of being dressed in white, having wings and singing for ever and ever in front of God's throne. Most people content themselves simply with the thought of the bliss of reunion.

But that means that there is no real bliss <u>before</u> reunion. Does that mean that we are longing for our healthy, happy loved ones to die and join us? Can we actually see their lives on earth? Can we see whether they are happy or not? Can we see them making the wrong choices? Do we suffer the frustration of not being able to help? Can we see them enduring the pain of our loss or other pains such as further bereavements or their own debilitating illnesses?

What kind of bliss is it to stand on the other side of the curtain of death completely unable to assist our partners, our children and grand-children and our friends when they need us?

Or am I in bliss because I have been completely cut off from the life of earth? Is my bliss simply the bliss of unconsciousness, of ignorance of all that is going on? But isn't that an empty and meaningless bliss?

Perhaps it is a bliss based on my own reunion with those who have gone before me, my grandparents, my parents, my siblings, my friends - even a child or two. And now I have the opportunity of meeting all those people I've always wanted to meet.

Do I have that opportunity? Suppose they don't want to meet me! And what about those people who used to pester me with their friendship on earth, a friendship I never reciprocated but was too polite to cut dead? What about the people I never want to see again even though for some unfathomable reason, they want to see me? And what about my pets? Will I see my hamster again?

So many questions and no answers. Fortunately for me, they don't bother me any more. As far as I am concerned, when I die I'm dead, and that's it. This life is all there is and I'm content with that.

WEEK 30

Trespassing

I have been reading Richard Adams' autobiography *The Day Gone By*. Richard Adams? The author of *Watership Down*, he lived near Newbury.

As an eight year old boy he went for a wander in the countryside and says that he was already conscious of the fact that if he wandered off the proper footpaths he was likely to be told off for trespassing.

From about that age I used to wander in the countryside on my own a good deal. I don't think it ever entered my head that land was actually owned by someone! Fields and woods were there just asking to be walked in.

And then when I was eleven I made friends with a number of farmer's sons. They all came from family farms and we used to walk them together. Now I became aware not only of ownership but of pride in the land. It was a welcoming pride. I still walked alone with perfect freedom.

But I suppose it must have been at about that age that I first became conscious of notices saying, *Keep Out - Trespassers will be prosecuted.* My father used to speak of a landowner who found that those notices were pretty useless so he put up a notice reading, *Beware of Snakes.* It always seemed to be the big landowners who wanted to keep people off the land. Perhaps the more you have, the more greedy you become and the more possessive.

I never took any notice of the notices. Someone had told me that the owners couldn't actually do anything to me except ask me to leave, provided I did no damage. I don't know whether that was true but I believed it - perhaps because I wanted to.

Throughout my life I have gone on behaving in the same way in a number of different counties. I've only been challenged three times so far. The first time I was on a public footpath close to a row of houses that led to fields and woods.

"Where do you think you're going?" came a very belligerent, hostile voice.

"I'm going for a walk," I replied equally forcefully.

I assumed that the grunt gave me permission to pass and I continued with my walk - but it left a nasty taste in the mouth and spoiled the afternoon.

On the second occasion I was walking in fields I had never been in, trying to find a way through that would enable me to get back home without retracing my steps. A lady hurtled across the fields on a quad, but this time I took the initiative.

"Are these your fields?" I asked, "only I'm trying to get back over there and there doesn't seem to be a way through."

Perhaps she would have been pleasant anyway, though the way she drove that quad makes me a bit doubtful, but when she knew that all I wanted to do was to get off her land, she became very friendly and helpful. I never took the risk of walking on her land again.

On the third occasion, Wendy and I had had a lovely walk along a bridle path through woodland. As we were thinking of turning back a man came across to us from where he was working. "You do realise that this is private property," he said. "No," I replied, "but we are about to turn back so we'll leave by the same gate that we came in by." And that was that.

Sometimes when we are out together Wendy will say to me, "Which farm do you think this land belongs to?"

"I've no idea," I answer. The truth is I'm not interested. While I'm on it, the land and the joy of being there belongs to me. Jesus said, "Blessed are the meek, for they shall inherit the earth." What a pity I'm not just that little bit more meek.

WEEK 31

The Greatest Bereavement

I have been forced to look again at the greatest failure of
my own life (nearly forty years ago) and to face it once
again. It is never far from the surface of my thoughts.

I did a great deal of harm and caused a great deal of pain
and I brought about the greatest bereavement of my own
life far worse than any death I have ever confronted. As a
result of my behaviour I lost the woman I loved, my children, my job (though I was invited to carry on with that),
and my wife.

Whatever all this meant for anybody else, I have never been
though such a hell (of my own making). I don't think it
would serve any useful purpose to spell out in detail what I
went through, or the continuing legacy of those years.

Starting again was extraordinarily difficult but the love and
support of my parents and brothers and my eldest brother's family, and the immediate help of a number of new
friends made it possible. And then Wendy (my second wife)
came on the scene and picked me up properly. My children
also played their part as they hung on to me and taught
me that I had not completely lost them though I had lost
any day to day involvement in their lives.

When I look back at those events and try to face up to
them squarely my reactions might prove to be surprising.

It will be no surprise to know that I would give a great deal
to have avoided causing so much hurt.

But I do not wish away those experiences of my life. I do
not wish away the love affair which, at the time, was

the deepest, richest and loveliest experience of my life. It taught me a great deal about the meaning of love.

Nor do I wish away my own pain in those days or my continuing pain. These have taught me a great deal about the emptiness and meaninglessness of religion; the depths of human resources and the crucial importance of standing on our own feet.

And they taught me that it is <u>always</u> possible to begin again and to build a new life. Anyone can make a new start. It helps no end if we are supported by love and friendship, but in the end it is down to us as individuals. As we succeed we rebuild our own self respect. Without a measure of self respect life is impossible. But each little step we take forward, each little thing we achieve, enables us to climb out of the ditch, to clean ourselves up and to face up to life again.

WEEK 32

Mystery and Knowledge

In Morris West's novel *The Shoes Of The Fisherman*, the Pope says,

"All life is a mystery, but the answer to the mystery is outside ourselves, and not inside. You can't go peeling yourself like an onion, hoping that when you come to the last layer you will find what an onion really is. At the end you are left with nothing."

It seems to me that this spells out precisely the great divide between Christianity and Humanism.

Humanists do not believe that life is a mystery except in the sense that it is something we only understand in part. That partial nature of our understanding is a challenge to us to strive to increase our knowledge and understanding.

Those who never peel an onion never get to know anything about an onion. They remain ignorant of its structure and of its capacity to make humans cry! They also remain ignorant of its value, of the way in which it can bring flavour and relish to a meal.

Similarly, if we never examine ourselves, never test ourselves, we never discover what we are or what our capacities are. We never discover the depths and riches of our own being. Nor do we discover the amazing truth that we have a usefulness for other people. The Pope in Morris's story suggests that in *demanding to know the explanation for everything we are committing an act of pride.* This is the old condemnation, laid at the door of Adam and Eve in the garden. They were forbidden to eat of *the tree of knowledge.*

Yet the truth is so often the reverse of this. It is the increase of knowledge which makes us humble because the more we know, the more we discover how little we know.

Christianity depends on convincing people that *all life is a mystery* and that it must remain that way.

Those who have the courage to nibble at the *tree of knowledge* may find themselves thrown out of the safe confines of the church's garden of Eden but they will also find that, perhaps for the first time, they are beginning to find their own feet, to stand on them as children learn to do, and to walk through life with head erect.

WEEK 33

Priesthood and Mystery

Every kind of priesthood sustains itself by convincing others that it holds the key to the mysteries of life and death.

By playing upon human ignorance, superstition and fear, the priest maintains his own place at or near the pinnacle of human society. Fortunately for the priest, ignorance, superstition and fear continue even in so-called civilised societies. As a result all kinds of priest, from the sophisticated Anglo-Catholic to the soothsayer, the astrologer and the medicine man, can maintain themselves in a safe, secure and comfortable life-style.

Many priests are convinced of the truth of the mysteries they purvey. At the heart of the faith of the Anglo-Catholic and of the Roman Catholic lies the mystery of the sacrifice of Christ re-enacted in the sacrament of his body and blood.

But what if (as many Christians believe) the bread is only bread and wine only wine?

The mystery has gone. The priesthood becomes literally the *priesthood of all believers.* The only mystery left is the mystery of the nature and purpose of God.

But what if there is no God?

Why then, there is no need for priests or for religion at all. We stand, ignorant still but without superstition or fear. We are no more than thinking, communicating animals living out our lives within the framework of the natural world. Because we are thinking animals, we strive to achieve the best lives we can. Because we are communicating animals we are also social animals. We find that what is best for the whole is also what is best for the individual.

Like all other living things, we are also breeding animals. This leads us to concern ourselves with what is best for future generations.

In all of this, we have no need for priests. Ignorance may persist but mystery is dead.

WEEK 34

A Philosophy Of Life

In letter XC of his *Letters from a Stoic* Seneca wrote to
Lucilius about the value of a philosophical approach to life.
He claimed that *living well is the gift of philosophy.*

My impression is that most of us live most of our lives in a
fairly unthinking way. Perhaps that is the only possible
way to live. We cannot spend every other moment examin-
ing ourselves, what we are doing, and why we are doing it.

But at the same time, the way we live our lives will be governed in a general sort of way by our philosophy of life -
our attitudes to ourselves, to those around us and to the
world in which we live.

So, even though too much introspection is unhealthy, it
remains important that we should take stock from time to
time and re-examine the fundamentals of the philosophy by
which we live. Seneca said that one doesn't go to anyone
other than oneself to find that philosophy of life.

He was both right and wrong!

Very few of us have the self-confidence or the arrogance to
feel that we need no teachers and some people never seem
to stop going from one teacher to another. I was once chatting with a highly qualified lady - perhaps in her forties.
She seemed to have explored just about every philosophy
under the sun. She was wondering where she should go
next. I said to her,

"Don't you think that it is about time that you stepped
back from all of this study and asked yourself where
YOUstand?"

The Buddha is a fine example of someone who went to all the teachers. But he didn't find enlightenment until he stopped and gave himself time to come to his own conclusions.

We can go to as many teachers as we like. We may find that all of them have been worthy of our attention. But we shall also find that none of them is infallible and there are times when some of them are seriously wrong. In the end, we need to make up our own minds about things.

We are free, independent adults. In childhood it may be good to play *follow my leader* but in adult life we have to work out our own philosophy of life.

"To thine own self be true."

WEEK 35

The Trouble With Ideology

During the first part of my life my experience of an ideology came from a Christianity to which I was totally committed, including a short spell as a missionary in India.

Christians do an immense amount of good all over the world. In my own area in India, they ran schools, hospitals, (erratic) health clinics and health education, and they engaged in agricultural work aimed at improving people's living standards.

All of that work demanded an organisation behind the people on the spot, an organisation that raised money and supported workers on the ground in every possible way. That organisation was, of course, the Christian Church and it did a great deal of good work.

But the supreme aim of the Christian Church is not to teach or to heal or to feed people. The supreme aim of the Christian Church is to make people Christian, to convert people and to win them for Christ, and that makes it divisive.

There is worse to come. Because Christians cannot agree amongst themselves and are themselves divided into a multitude of different sects, they replicate their divisions throughout the world. So their religion makes them divisive and the divided nature of their religion makes them even more divisive.

If we are to succeed in dealing with problems of world dimensions, there has to be organisation. But organisations are needed that are not driven by any ideology, and fortunately there are plenty around.

They are driven by warmth of humanity, a desire for justice and fair play, a longing for peace, and similar human qualities. But alongside all these things is an acceptance of other people as they are in all their diversity.

Whatever their race, religion, culture, civilisation, they are simply regarded as fellow human beings whose needs are greater than our own and often desperately so.

So, where the missionary spirit or ideology is divisive and can even be dangerous, the heart of compassion and the human hand of friendship are unifying. Ordinary humanity and fellow feeling can overcome all divisions and leap across them, healing humanity's wounds and binding us all together in a mutual quest for a good life for all humankind.

WEEK 36

Symbols

Since the rumpus over the Cross at a Devonshire crematorium, I have had a number of letters asking me about my attitude to symbols (and telling me what my correspondents think.)

In my lifetime attitudes have changed as radically as society itself. In the 1950s a new clergyman came to the village in Lancashire where I lived. He placed a plain wooden cross on the altar of his Church. It was something new!

He was denounced as a papist. Some people stopped going to his church and others moved to the Methodist Church. But within a few years the Methodist church had a wooden cross too! There was considerable debate about it and unease. In the 1960s when I was living in Derbyshire many non-conformists and Methodists still thought of even a plain wooden cross as *a graven image* forbidden by the bible. They thought of it as an emblem of idolatry.

Are there Christians who still think in those terms? If they felt that way about a plain wooden cross, imagine how they felt about a crucifix, a cross with an image of the crucified Christ on it. That really was idolatrous and papist. Yet I know of one crematorium where the central symbol is a crucifix. They don't have a plain cross. The manager tells me that in his time there, he has never had a complaint from a non-conformist or Methodist minister.

Times have clearly changed and I suspect that most people would simply wonder what all the fuss is about.

Have you ever visited a really old graveyard owned by the local authority? Part of it was reserved for members of the Church Of England. And part of it was reserved for Roman

Catholics. A third section was reserved for non-conformists and Methodists. And somewhere discreet and out of the way a small patch was reserved for paupers, suicides and non-Christians. Local authorities were ashamed of this section and kept it as much out of sight as possible. The fact that some people were beyond the pale was not something they wanted to advertise.

But in today's society something like 40% of us belong to that beyond the pale group and although we don't want to make too much fuss about it, we do want to be treated properly. One place where we should be treated properly is a crematorium or a cemetery chapel.

Most crematoria were built at a time when Christianity was still the dominant religion in the country and Christian symbols were included as a matter of course. But those symbols are inappropriate for people of other religions - for Buddhists, Confucians, Hindus, Moslems, Taoists and so on. They are also inappropriate for those of us who have no religion at all.

WEEK 37

A Failure At School?

A number of my friends have been friends ever since we were at school together. One of them once achieved 5% in a maths exam *for neatness*. He wrote the title of the exam and his name on the top of the first sheet and then underlined them. And he managed all this without making a single blot! Then he sat back and allowed his vivid imagination to wander.

In a maths lesson he once asked our teacher what practical use maths had. The teacher made no attempt to answer him but just went on with his lesson. He wasn't a bad teacher. After all, he got me through school certificate maths! But I suspect that his lessons were all mapped out, to be followed year after year without alteration and certainly without interruption. His own mind was probably away with his model railways.

I have often wondered what we were doing in that maths lesson. Was it algebra? I used to like algebra. There was something satisfying and neat about a = this and b = that and so on. Of course a doesn't actually = anything except a and b doesn't = anything except b. But I wasn't aware of that at the time, nor did I ask my friend's question. But I have never used algebra since I left school.

My own particular bête noir came in science lessons when we were supposed to learn the scientific letters for things. The only one I ever learned was H_2O for water. But I've never needed these things since leaving school. However, let us return to my old school friend:

Needless to say, between school and National Service in the army, my friend worked in a bank!

He went on to have a varied career including a spell in the Canadian Mounties. Did he ever get his man? In school games he was usually on the other side, full of skilful inventiveness when it came to preventing us from finding him.

But his lack of ability at maths obviously bugged him. There came a time when he was determined to crack the nut. And this time he found a teacher who was able to help him through whatever mental block was there. So successful was he that he ultimately became a teacher himself -of maths of course.

It isn't actually true to call my friend 'a failure at school.' His only failure was in maths. But I've known others who just never got on with their teachers for a variety of different reasons and who were written off with pretty awful school leaving reports. But once away from 'compulsory education' they found their feet and made their successful way in life.

There is a degree to which schools, of necessity, have to be 'one size fits all' establishments, and there is always focus on academic prowess. But one size doesn't fit all, and academic prowess or book learning doesn't actually fit very many.

There is an old story of a visiting American Indian chief who wondered what on earth we were doing, packing our children off to school at the very time when they needed to be learning! Whether with a successful schooling or not, we have to find our own way through the school of life. That is the hardest examination of all.

WEEK 38

Faith and Independent Schools

My elder brothers went to state schools. So did I until the second world war broke out. Then I had a year in a Catholic school, academically at least a year behind my council school. Ultimately I ended up in a small Methodist boarding school and then after National Service in the Navy, to a small Methodist Theological College which was a part of London University but lived its life virtually without reference to the University.

I enjoyed schooling. I also enjoyed my time at Theological College although I had had quite enough by the time I left. I can't see that either experience did me any harm except that, but for the Navy, my experience of life was exceptionally narrow - almost exclusively Methodist.

The boarding school WAS small. There were less than 120 of us when I joined and not all that many more when I left. In theory that should have made for close staff-pupil relationships and for a good academic education. In practice the education was probably neither better nor worse than at state schools and I only ever wanted to keep in touch with one member of staff after I left.

Yet I had been happy enough to want my sons to follow me there. It was only in retrospect that I changed my mind and wanted them to grow up in a world where there were both boys and girls! That didn't necessarily mean that they had to have co-ed schools but they did have to live in a world where it was possible to meet girls in a normal way as they grew up.

In the 1950s I worked in an area close to Preston in Lancashire. The village I lived in had three all-age schools.

One was Church of England. One was Methodist. One was Roman Catholic. The first two played games against one another but they had no relationship with the third. Roman Catholics and Protestants did not mix. Nor did their parents except when they had to, at work or on the local council. Luckily there was no real hostility but there was a mild underlying, suspicion and even dislike.

For the first time I found myself thinking about the provision of education in this country and the chaos we have inherited from the past. I began to ask myself what State Educational Provision should be.

And then came de-segregation laws in the USA and all that went with those; apartheid in South Africa; and the troubles in Northern Ireland. Added to that, there was a growing immigrant population in our own country with widely differing backgrounds, cultures and religions.

Whether we like it or not, people will segregate themselves up to a point, gathering in comfort clusters among those with whom they feel safest and most comfortable. But increasingly I came to see that nothing that the State does should in anyway encourage or enhance the divisions that exist in society. And it is that conviction that has come to underline my own convictions about state education. It is the duty of the State to provide the best secular education it can for all of its citizens and that is its ONLY responsibility. It is not the job of the government to subsidise either the wealthy or the religious. If people want to opt out of the State system they should be free to do so but not with the support of tax payers money.

If Christians or Jews or Muslims want schools of their own, let them have them but let them also fund them. If the wealthy want to segregate their children from the rest of society in an Eton or a Harrow or something a little less, let them do so, but let them also fund them.

If my views were implemented, I suspect that the number of independent schools would dwindle rapidly. But we would also have a large number of parents determined that State provision would be uniformly good and that would prove more salutary and more valuable than all the political babble we have endured about *education, education, education.*

WEEK 39

In The Image Of God

I don't know how he found me but one of my old tutors began writing to me and sent me a copy of his poems. Many of them are about the life and work of Jesus and in one of them he talks about the worth of a human being.

He claims that it is the fact that we are made "in the image of God" that gives us our worth. As I read the poem I remembered listening to a prayer that amused me so much that I may have mentioned it before:

"Oh God, we thank thee for Ethel. We thank thee that thou hast made her in thine own image. We thank thee for her love of Bingo."

My tutor's poem set me thinking. The idea that humans have been singled out by God to be made in his image seems to me to be the source of a great deal of erroneous thinking about our place in the world and our relationship with the rest of the natural world. It puts us on a pedestal as if we were somehow more special than anything else. It claims that we are special to God in a unique way, not shared by anything else.

Since I do not believe in God, I do not share that opinion. We may be special to ourselves but as far as the rest of the world is concerned, we are only special because we have become especially dangerous. So often our creative powers are used at the expense of the world we live in.

With a touch more humility we might begin to learn that our supreme responsibility is to learn to live as lightly as we can and as much in harmony with everything else as is possible. For everything in the world is inter-related and everything we do affects other people and other creatures.

The people of greatest worth are not those who leave the deepest footprint behind them but often those who pass almost unnoticed through the world.

The BBC runs fairly silly programmes about 'unsung heroes,' but behind the silliness and sentimentality there is a genuine truth. It is not those who hit the headlines who are necessarily the most valuable human beings, but those who live their lives quietly and well, without any fuss at all. One anonymous author wrote:

"Not, how did he die, but how did he live?
Not, what did he gain, but what did he give?
These are the units to measure the worth
Of a man as a man, regardless of birth.
Not what was his church, nor what was his creed?
But had he befriended those really in need?
Was he ever ready, with word of good cheer,
To bring back a smile, to banish a tear?

Not what did the sketch in the newspaper say,
But how many were sorry when he passed away?"

Some years ago I played about with a Buddhist piece and finally came up with the following:

Let those of us who seek the good,
who know the meaning of the place of peace,
abandon vain discussions
and go forward with clarity of vision.

Let us be alive, upright and sincere,
without conceit of self,
easily contented and joyous,
free of cares.
Let us not be submerged by the things of the world,
let our senses be controlled,
let us avoid the puffing up of pride,
let us do nothing that is mean or that the wise would

reprove.

Let none deceive another or despise another,
let none by anger or ill-will wish harm to another,
Rather let us be happy and at our ease,
let us be joyous and live in friendship with one another.

Let us cherish all living things,
let us cultivate a boundless goodwill,
radiating friendship over the entire world.

In other words, let us try to be decent human beings
living in harmony with the rest of the world of nature.
We don't need to single ourselves out or to imagine
that we are anything special.

WEEK 40

Child Abuse And Under Age Sex

The newspapers love stories of rape and child abuse, perhaps especially child abuse. With their mock, shocked horror morality and their delight in titillating nastiness and in stirring up witch hunts, they can't get enough of it.

But when we come face to face with such things, we need to be extraordinarily careful. This is a world where all is seldom as it seems.

That there is child abuse and that it is horrible and evil and unforgivable is undeniable. I have no wish to underestimate or to underplay the sheer nastiness of all this.

But we should be very careful not to confuse child abuse and under-age sex. We should also be extremely careful before we condemn adults who have sex with youngsters who are under the legal age for sex. Where sex is concerned, the legal age has very little to do with things.

In days gone by families often all slept in the same bed. We used to sing the round, "there were ten in a bed and the little one said, Roll Over, and they all rolled over and one fell out. There were nine in a bed....."

In those circumstances it would be amazing if sometimes things didn't go wrong. Many years ago I wrote about a cockney family:

"I'm sorry Glad,
I thought yer was yer mother.
That's alright dad,
I thought yer was me brother."

Nowadays almost all children have their own beds and boys and girls usually have separate bedrooms, so that kind of accident is unlikely to occur which means that incestuous relationships are almost always deliberate on one side or the other. The same is also true of any other relationship between an adult and an underage youngster.

But what do I mean by 'on one side or the other?' We are very quick to condemn the adults involved in such relation-ships. But there are an awful lot of children who have the art of seduction off to a fine art when they are still very young. Given an adult who is weak enough or foolish enough they are quite capable of playing the leading role. And a few of them are nasty enough to put the adult through the hell of revelation afterwards. So we need to be very careful before we condemn.

There are other adult/child relationships which can be thoroughly beneficial to both. Wealthy fathers used to send their sons (always their sons) to France to 'complete their education!' How many bored housewives have begun the sexual initiation and education of a boy whose 'balls have dropped.' There are many men who are grateful for the guiding hand of an older woman when they were young, and many more of us who wish we had had such a guiding hand. Do women stop to ask whether the boy is 14 or 16? Should they be condemned for a relationship with a 14 year old and praised for the same relationship with a 16 year old?

Praised?

If it is helpful to the lad, why not?

And what are we to make of the youthful fumblings of the young themselves? Untidy, chaotic, often embarrassing but these are a part of the learning process. When things work out they simply become 'a bit of fun' often leading to 'going too far' when excitement overwhelms them both. It's no use condemning them when things go wrong and unwanted, unexpected pregnancies ensue.

So: 'they should have been more careful. They should have taken precautions.'

Did they know in advance that their petting would lead to this? Of course not. And again, what difference does it make whether they are 14 or 16? The legal age is irrelevant when they become sexually active.

Condemnation helps no one. We simply have to be there for them, surrounding them with our love and understanding and helping them to find their own best way through.

In the whole area of this desperate minefield of sex with or among the young, each separate, individual case needs careful, thoughtful and understanding examination. Only the genuinely nasty, ruthless, evil people deserve our condemnation and the punishment of society. But the rest deserve no publicity and sometimes gratitude and sometimes help, and always friendliness and understanding.

Post-script: Oddly enough, the day before I read this through in preparation for sending it off to the publisher I visited a family where the parents began their relationship when the girl was 13. Yes, it was a sexual relationship. But it was much more than that. They married as soon as she was 16 and had a successful marriage and family.

WEEK 41

An Atheist And An Epicurean

I have often wondered why it is that people dislike the word *atheist* so much. It has always seemed to me to be a pretty innocuous, inoffensive word, just a simple denial of belief in God.

I suppose that for god-fearing people and for the superstitious that is all it takes. The denial of belief in gods is enough to make people fear and hate you. Strange!

I understand rather better why Christians have always shown such hostility towards the teachings of Epicurus and why they have twisted and perverted them. Long before Jesus came onto the scene, Epicurus offered a simple, all-inclusive philosophy that in some respects was streets ahead of Christianity both as it was in its early days and as it is now. His philosophy was quietist, welcoming and open to all - young and old, male and female, slave and free - and all on equal terms. Epicurus based his philosophy firmly on the concept of the rich possibilities of human friendship. He saw the gods as an irrelevance and was thoroughly this-worldly in his approach.

And there you have it: for the god-fearing and the superstitious, that is quite enough to make people fear and hate you.

But that kind of paranoia has a very specific history in Britain. It was a paranoia fed by Governments and led to a whole series of irrational associations which have nothing to do with atheism at all. Yet they persist in the background and still form an undercurrent in Government thinking and decision making. If we want to understand we have to go back in time.

The Renaissance and the Reformation between them set the intellectual world and the religious world of Europe in a ferment. As always, there was a great deal of confusion and a great deal of mixing things together in people's minds, things that didn't belong together. There was also a great deal of misinformation and excessive governmental paranoia.

(Governments and the media are experts at creating and feeding off paranoia as the issues of violent crime and terrorism today make clear.)

In Elizabethan times the main paranoia concerned the Catholic threat to our Protestant Country and to the Queen, a threat that was real enough. As in Roman Times, what the Government wanted was outward conformity to the State and to the State Religion, a conformity marked by attendance at church on Sunday. As long as people conformed they could believe what they liked and there do seem to have been many closet atheists.

What the Government didn't want was the open expression of anything other than the State Religion. It didn't want Catholics and it didn't want Non-conformists and it didn't want atheists. Of these, Catholics were obvious dangers because some of them really were involved in plots against the crown. But because they didn't toe the conformist line both non-conformists and atheists were somehow thought to be unpatriotic.

Ex President Bush is only the latest in a long line of those who denounce anyone who opposes the Government line. Conformity and patriotism have nothing to do with one another. Indeed it is often those who do not conform who are actually the best patriots. But disconnected and irrational thinking run right through this subject.

In Government eyes nonconformists and atheists demonstrated at very least a willingness to rock the boat and a rebellious spirit. In Tudor times atheism was also associated with an Epicureanism which was perverted by being seen through the hostile lens of Christian antagonism and propaganda. But now see what happens.

Epicurus was Greek. Greek society was tolerant of homosexual behaviour. Therefore atheists were homosexuals (!) or at very least, accepting of homosexuals. And homosexuality was anathema to Catholics too but that fact somehow became lost as the argument progressed.

For another of the things that made atheists dangerous was that they were republicans and therefore a threat to the Queen. Certainly some of them were republicans but it doesn't follow that they would engage in plots to bring the monarchy down with violence. I'm a republican myself but I don't offer a threat to anyone. Michael Foot was a republican but it didn't stop him getting on well with the Queen and her mother.

However, let us see the final absurdity as we look at where their arguments finally took Tudor Governments. Because atheists are republicans they are obviously the natural allies of Roman Catholics! How absurd can you get? But all these were arguments and ideas churned out by Government and State Church alike in order to discredit atheists.

When you see how long it takes for people to leave bad history, bad ideas and wrong-headed thinking behind, it becomes possible to understand the continuing hostility to atheism which in itself is harmless, and to Epicureanism which is one of the loveliest and most inclusive philosophies the world has ever seen.

WEEK 42

The Trouble With Labels

If we go to a conference, one of the first things we are asked to do is to put a label on so that we know who we are.

We label people in a host of different ways: by colour, by nationality, by political party, by religion or irreligion and by a host of clubs and organisations of all kinds.

Labels have their usefulness in telling us a little bit about one another. But there are dangers in labels. They can be exclusive and they can be divisive. They can also lead us to pigeon hole people and to put them into a box which is too small for them. We tend to assume that all those people who are wearing the same label can be defined in the same way. But that is only true in terms of minimum definitions. Try putting all those with Christian in their lapels into one box and see what terrible trouble you would be in.

In fact, Christians themselves tried it. They established the world council of churches. But right from the beginning there were major churches that wouldn't join and when they tried to define the Christianity of those who did join they had to whittle the definition down and down until they were left with just one sentence of shared belief. Nor would they all have put the same meaning on the words of that one sentence.

Because human beings are two kinds of animal at the same time our lives are lived in a constant state of tension.

We are social animals. As a result, as we pass through life, we tend to look around for like-minded people who will provide us with comradeship and a comforting sense of security. We are not alone in a hostile world.

When I did my National Service we had to be labelled by religion. I gave mine as *Methodist* which led a complete stranger to say to me "Thank God I've found another Methodist!" As it happens we've been friends ever since even though I left Methodism many years ago. But finding someone with a similar background in the frightening surroundings of a naval *ship* in the heart of Wiltshire gave a sense of comfort and security.

There is a centripetal force which draws us towards one another into family and group relationships.

But in addition to being social animals, each one of us is also a unique individual. Not even identical twins are totally alike. And this means that we often become uncomfortable in the groups we have joined. This is especially true of highly centralised groups where distant authority figures try to impose their will on us. They want to be the people who define the label we are wearing but our own definition is rather different. So there is also a centrifugal force which pulls many of us away from the centre and often out of the group altogether.

Sometimes this leads us simply to assert our independence and individuality and to sit quietly on the sidelines. Some times we find that we are lonely again so we look around for another group where we can find companionship and happiness. And sometimes we actually go so far as to set about establishing a new group of our own.

You only have to look at the local paper to see what a multitude of groups there are. And always there are new groups forming and old groups disbanding. All this is simply a sign of the life and vigour of human society. There is nothing to worry about in this ferment of change unless groups are secretive or exclusive or in some way anti-social and destructive.

One of the problems with both religious and non-religious organisations (including political parties) is that whilst most of them long to be inclusive, almost all of them end up being exclusive. Perhaps the nearest thing to a genuinely inclusive religion is Hinduism which does its best to be all things to all men - a kind of umbrella religion in which we can all shelter. There have been modern attempts to do away with all previous religions and to gather the best from all religions into one organisation, but all that they have succeeded in doing is adding one more to the total list.

I grew up within the evangelical Christian tradition where the evangelical essence of the movement had run out of steam. Nevertheless I was brought up to believe that if only we could convert the whole world to Christianity through the missionary work of the church, we would establish a perfect world.

This was not only a pipe-dream. It was also the source of a great deal of hostility and conflict. When I went to live in India one of the commonest graffiti simply said, "Get out Christian Missionaries." You do not get on with other people by trying to convert them to your own point of view whether in religion or politics or anything else. You get on with people by accepting them as they are, as unique, independent, adult human beings with the same capacity for friendship as your own.

The one thing we all have in common is our humanity. If we make that our starting point with other people we shall almost always be able to get on with them and we shall often be able to move beyond "getting on with them" to genuine friendship.

In my work I used to be labelled as a Methodist minister and there was a time when I was proud of that label. For rather more than the last thirty years I have been labelled as a Humanist Celebrant and again , I am proud of the label. But if either label ever came between me and the service I wished to offer to other people I preferred to scrap the label.

If I can be friends with someone or useful to someone that is enough. Their labels and mine are completely irrelevant. As a result I have been able to serve people of the Bahai faith, Buddhists, Confucians, Jews, Muslims, Pagans and a host of people whose views are non-specific and undefined. This is as it should be. Behind all labels we are just people.

WEEK 43

"In Heaven There is no Marrying or Giving in Marriage." (Jesus)

Why is that I wonder?

We know so little of heaven. In fact, let's be honest, we know nothing of heaven. We don't know where it is or what it is like, unless we are male Muslim terrorists, and there aren't anywhere near as many of those as the Government try to tell us. They know that heaven awaits them, a rather sensual heaven full of houris, nymphs whose delights were never available on earth.

Christians know about heaven too. It seems to be full of cherubs and angels and harps and singing, but no tubas apparently. And there is an awful lot of white. We're told that we can gaze and gaze and gaze upon the face of God because we are going to spend a great deal of time standing before his throne.

But is there a reunion with loved ones from earth? That seems to be the supreme human hope and yet on that there's not a word - not one solitary word to encourage us in that belief or hope.

But there is some good news. Paul tells us that we shall have new bodies - that can't be bad, especially for those of us who die in old age. Our new bodies will be spiritual bodies, whatever that may mean. It looks as though they will be no good for sex or even close companionship for there's no marrying in heaven. We have it on the authority of Jesus himself.

Why I wonder?

Is it because marriage is such a supreme human relationship that it separates us from other human relationships to a degree, if only by becoming the pre-eminent relationship of our lives? And in heaven no relationship must mean more than any other?

Or is it because our marriage companions become so important to us that, though we fully recognise one another's faults, we are still inclined to think of one another with something approaching worship and in heaven that will never do? Nothing must deflect us from our total, everlasting, all-consuming worship of God whom we now see face to face.

Of course, marriage can be pretty awful. But on the other hand, perhaps Jesus the bachelor spoke as he did because he never knew that a really good marriage is heavenly!

There are a large number of religious people who have a rather different take on this heaven business. After a series of lives on earth in different guises and with no memory linking the lives to one another, at last we find the way to the supreme bliss of dissolution as we are swallowed up and gathered back into the ALL from which or whom we first emerged.

That doesn't seem all that far removed from the simple view that when we die, creatures of the natural world that we are, we return to nature for re-cycling! And if that is true, we'd better do our best to ensure that we enjoy our heaven here.

WEEK 44

The Crusades

In 1987 Radio 4 ran a series called "The Cross and the Crescent" which was intended to be a popular history of the crusades. I didn't hear the series at the time but I have read the book by Malcolm Billings. Since then ex President Bush opened his can of worms by speaking in crusading terms of the invasion of Iraq and the unspeakable horrors that unleashed.

Perhaps we have become more sensitive since then. Certainly the 2008 TV series by Boris Johnson gave proper respect to the Muslim side of the Muslim/Christian divide. But I was amazed at how slanted Malcolm Billings *history* was.

During the first crusade at the end of the 1000s AD Roman Catholic Christians managed to carve out for themselves a number of states running around the north-eastern corner of the Mediterranean all the way down the eastern coast from Antioch down to and including Jerusalem. Their military successes were marked by all the horrors invading armies commonly inflict on non-combatant civilian populations.

From the time of the first crusade onwards the crusaders consistently lost ground to Muslim armies until they were finally driven out of the eastern half of the Mediterranean altogether. Yet the book, although it cannot ignore these facts, focuses entirely on such few crusader victories as there were. And it plays down two further facts:

Successful Muslim armies were far more disciplined towards civilian populations than Christian armies, although there were plenty of horror stories on both sides.

What is more, when treaties were made, Muslims tended to keep them but Christians tended to break faith.

Apart from the crusades in the middle east, the only other crusade against Muslims was in Spain where Christian might slowly prevailed and where Christian leaders behaved despicably towards both Muslims and Jews. This contrasts badly with the fact that for centuries, Muslim leaders had behaved with a fair measure of tolerance towards both Jews and Christians.

All other crusades were crusades by Roman Catholic Christians against other Christians: orthodox Christians in Constantinople and *heretics* elsewhere.

In the midst of all this, Malcolm Billings does his best to focus on nobility, sacrifice, heroism and so on - mostly on Christians who displayed these virtues. But because he can't avoid including a good deal of genuine history from the period, it is impossible to hide the fact that the crusades were sordid, callous and cruel. Their primary purpose was to bring added power to the papacy and their secondary purpose was to bring wealth to the leading crusaders and to cities such as Venice.

Venice did have a genuine grievance against Constantinople where there had been a terrible slaughter of Venetians not all that long before the crusade concerned.

But this doesn't alter the fact that the crusades were some of the most vile and shameful episodes in the history of christendom. The religion of the *Prince Of Peace* has a great deal to answer for. And now, of course, it is the terrorist wing of Islam which is adding to the evil story of religious bigotry and the carnage to which it leads.

None of this takes anything away from the marvels of art, architecture, literature and so on that express the very best of human achievement in both Christian and Muslim societies. But it does all make me very thankful that, rather late in the day, I renounced Christianity and indeed all religion.

Again and again in my dealings with other people I find that it is the nasty and evil things done in the name of religion that turn people off, just as the nasty and evil things done in the name of our country make us ashamed again and again of British governments.

WEEK 45

War

For many people the invasion of Iraq was a wake-up call. It is now widely seen to have been both morally wrong and sheer folly. The death toll has been enormous and there has been widespread devastation. My MP, who voted for war, now admits that he was wrong. He is not alone.

People are now beginning to admit that having soldiers in Afghanistan is achieving nothing but loss of life and horrific injuries. It is not reducing drug traffic and it is not defeating the Taliban nor does it in anyway reduce the dangers of terrorism elsewhere in the world.

Even Winston Churchill, who was hardly the most pacific of our prime ministers, wrote from Afghanistan when he was there with our troops as a young man, to say that although our troops were doing well, they were wasting their time and effort and achieving nothing.

I take no pride in the fact that I was one of the many who saw these things from the outset and did my little best to protest. We have been shown to be right but we were both helpless and ineffective when faced with a prime minister bent on war.

Looking back over my life it seems to me that most wars could have and should have been avoided. They are so often caused by failures in diplomacy and negotiation, by an unwillingness to find paths of compromise and agreement. Or they are caused by having the wrong people in power, trigger-happy, power-hungry demagogues who can talk the talk safe in the knowledge that they will never serve on the front line themselves. There ought to be a law requiring all those who vote for any war to be immediately placed in the first line of attack or defence, the first line of fighting troops. And they should be the last to be supplied with whatever inadequate equipment the ministry of defence is handing out.

Growing up in the Second World War, I have never quite been able to say that ALL wars are wrong. But there is no doubt that most wars are preventable. With hindsight we can see that different behaviour after the First World War would have given us a different Germany with no room for a Hitler to find power and so no need for a Second World War. All the nations involved in the post world war one settlement share responsibility for the rise of Hitler and the Second World War.

A friend of mine who was a devout Christian decided to study the Christian doctrine of the just war for her doctorate. Ultimately she came to the conclusion that there is no such thing and her thesis was published, I think by the Lutterworth Press. This led her to a lifetime of service in the cause of peace.

In her 80s she published one final volume called *A Pilgrimage Towards Peace* published by Sessions of York. At the same time as I was reading Joan Simkins' book I was also reading John Ellis' book about *The Fighting Man In World War II*. Only about one in five soldiers in the British Army were actually involved in combat 'at the sharp end.' The story of all that they endured is so terrible that I had to force myself to go on reading.

It struck me that all the academic arguments in the world will never stop us fighting one another. And since, as I mentioned earlier, politicians and diplomats are never the people who actually experience life at the sharp end, the experience of ordinary soldiers is not likely to stop war either.

When the huge peace rallies failed to stop Tony Blair invading Iraq as George Bush's underling, it is difficult to see what will stop wars. We need a completely changed mind-set but where will it come from. My correspondence with my local MP leaves me thoroughly pessimistic. But if there is to be a changed mind-set it can only come from the continuing struggle against the odds of all those who love peace and hate war.

It needs to be drummed in to the minds and hearts of all politicians and would-be politicians the world over that war must ALWAYS be the very last option to be considered.

I have just read this through prior to sending it off for publication - just after the Israelites have inflicted three weeks of terror, horror and destruction in Gaza. The horrors of the Holocaust over sixty years ago still seem to inhibit us all from condemning such Israeli actions as forcefully as we should.

Without in any way denying the evil of those who fire rockets from Palestine, it is high time that someone had the guts to denounce what has become one of the most brutal and inhuman nations on earth. What Israel has done and is doing in Gaza is just as bad in its way as the Holocaust, even more impersonal, just as horrific and just as wrong and it should be condemned as such without any hesitation or looking over the shoulder at Jewish voters elsewhere in the world.

Evil is evil wherever it is found and no matter what the provocation. It should be roundly condemned as such.

WEEK 46

Is This Our Last Millennium?

Over 90% of all species that have ever lived are now extinct.

Through most of the world's history the loss of species through extinction has been compensated for by the fact that more species have been evolving so that the sheer number of species has been growing. But there have been six periods when that position has been reversed.

The best known came at the end of the Cretaceous period when the dinosaurs and over three quarters of all other species became extinct.

The last of these six periods is now and humans are the cause. Our exploitation of the world in which we live has grown apace. Farming has always exploited the land but the development of industrial agriculture during the 20th century has made it the greatest culprit in our decimation of our world. But let me hasten to add that most farmers are as much victims of the system as anybody else. They are no more and no less culpable than the rest of us.

As more and more of us have been driven off the land, our consumerism has aggravated the problem and hastened the crisis. It is our cities that are primarily responsible for climate change. But this week I want to focus on our loss of bio-diversity.

From agriculture through to the supermarkets there is a consistent narrowing of options, a consistent reduction in the bio-diversity not only of our own locality but of the world as a whole.

Surely not? As we wander round the supermarkets we are filled with wonder at the way in which we are spoiled for choice. There are so many things there that our forefathers could never have dreamed of buying at their local grocers' shop.

If we think that way let us look again. One simple and obvious example must suffice. How many different varieties of apple does your supermarket stock? Now travel a couple of hundred miles across country and visit a different super-market - Safeway instead of Sainsbury, Tesco instead of Waitrose. How many varieties of apple are there? A similar number? The SAME varieties? What has happened to the rich diversity of our childhood?

Agriculture has always been selective. It has always grown more of less: a greater quantity of fewer species. The development of industrial agriculture has hastened that process using fewer varieties of fruit; fewer types of vegetable; fewer grain-yielding grasses; fewer breeds of cattle, sheep, pigs - always more of less. The development of GM foods is one more step along the same path.

As agricultural diversity shrinks, all those inter-related and inter-dependent elements of the natural world shrink with it - even without the destructive use of pesticides and chemical fertilisers.

Our exploitation of the world for profit today is destroying the world. Already 20% of the world's fresh-water fish are extinct or in danger of extinction.

Does It Matter?

Does it matter to the city dweller if the song of the skylark is never heard again? Does it matter if my grandchild never sees or hears a thrush? What they have never known they will never miss. Does it matter?

I read somewhere the suggestion that we should imagine a ship. One of the rivets comes loose and falls into the sea. Nobody notices. Other rivets follow and still nobody notices. Then the day comes when a sheet of steel from the hull falls off and the ship sinks. How many lost rivets did it take? How many lost species does it take to destroy enough of the bio-diversity of the world to lead to disaster?

Nobody knows. So even if we don't care about a single species like a skylark or a thrush, simple self-preservation should begin to make us take care. Unless we wish to see humanity bring itself a disaster similar in extent to that which befell the dinosaurs and most other life with them we need to change direction and to change direction fast.

In Scandinavia people are heavily dependent on their forests. They have learned the art of sustainable forestry, restricting and replacing all that they take. This is not because they are more virtuous than the rest of us. It is a simple act of self preservation.

Over the whole agricultural landscape of the world we need to learn the same lessons. For thousands of years at an accelerating rate and now at breackneck speed, we have been taking, taking, taking from the world with little thought of the consequences of our greed.

Now with billions of people in the world, it may be already too late but we can at least try to ensure that it is not. We can't turn the clock back but the time has more than come when exploitation must be matched and more than matched by restoration. The industrial wastelands must be brought back to life; the rivers and the seas allowed to recover from our depredations; and the land to support its natural diversity of living things.

WEEK 47

Harmony with Nature

"We must recognise that it is nature, not man, that is omniscient on the earth, but that if we continue to flout Nature's laws, humanity may not have a future."

No this is not the same week or thought as the last one. But it is similar. When I look back over the things I have written about in recent years, one of the most consistent themes expresses a concern for the world in which we live.

When people lived closer to the land they understood more about the way nature works than urban dwellers of today's world. They may have developed a host of myths and legends to try to imbue nature with a spirituality it doesn't possess, but they all understood very well that if we mess about with our natural environment we are storing up trouble for ourselves. And so they all taught respect for the world and for all the creatures in it.

You will find this kind of respect in the ancient Indian religions such as Hinduism, Jainism and Buddhism and you will find it amongst all sorts of 'primitive' peoples throughout the world including the Maoris of Australia and New Zealand and the American Indians.

But you find the opposite in the three Judaic religions which take much of their teaching from the bible. Many years ago C S Lewis wrote "Atheists naturally regard the co-existence of man and the other animals as a mere contingent result of interacting biological facts; and the taming of an animal by man as a purely arbitrary interference of one species with another. The real or natural animal to them is the wild one, and the tame animal is an artificial or unnatural thing.

But a Christian must not think so. Man was appointed by
God to have dominion over the beasts."

Those two simple sentences expose the Biblical teaching
which has been fundamental to many of the evils of industrial farming of which I wrote last week. But the extent of
the devastation runs far wider than farming. It runs
through the whole of human life. In my lifetime it has been
seen as least as badly in the spreading of towns and cities
into the countryside and in the smothering of countryside
with new roads and motorways.

As town and city-dwellers we have lost touch with our
roots. We fail to understand that the natural world is an
indivisible unity of which we are a fairly insignificant part.
Those who read John Donne's famous poem *No Man Is An
Island* remember his line *Any man's death diminishes me*
but easily by-pass the verse which begins *If a clod be
washed away by the sea, Europe is the less.*

We corrupt and cover the land; we destroy the forests; we
pollute the environment at our peril. Schauberger, whose
quotation began this week, was *passionate about trees. He
warned that deforestation would deplete the world of water
and destroy fertility, causing deserts and climatic chaos.*

Since Schauberger I have read others who are equally concerned about our mis-use of water. They also paint a very
bleak picture of trouble ahead. We are busy *sowing the
wind* and we shall inevitably *reap the whirlwind.*

Urgently we need to learn to live in harmony with the rest
of nature and to have a proper respect for everything
around us. Unless we do, much of the natural world is
doomed and in the end, we are doomed with it.

I suspect that we ARE doomed. I don't really believe deep
down that we have the humility, the understanding or the
will to turn from our folly and to see sense. We have

become the most destructive species on earth and in the end, we shall destroy ourselves.

Is the message a total message of doom and gloom? Probably! But hopeless though it may be, we can at very least seek in our own lives to recognise our interdependence; to live respectfully and with genuine consideration for all other living things; and so to live as lightly as we can upon the earth. And all the time we can press our governments to reduce the harm they do and to begin and continue to work for the healing of the earth.

WEEK 48

Changing Times

My father was an employer. When the wife of one of his employees was sick, he cared enough about them to pay a visit. He took one of my brothers with him. The man offered my dad a cup of tea and offered my brother a cup of cocoa. My brother was delighted but when the cocoa came he had a bit of a shock.

There was no milk and no sugar. It was the first time in his life that he was aware of the financial hardships many families faced. He obviously wasn't aware of the fact that one of our grandmothers used to wait until late on Friday and then go to the market to pick up things that were being sold off cheap. She also had a struggle to make ends meet without actually being in poverty.

It was evacuation which opened my eyes, not so much to other people's poverty as to the differences in people's lives. For the first time I lived in houses where there was no electric light. The ones I lived in had gas lighting but I visited homes where there wasn't gas either and oil lamps were used. Some of the houses I lived in had no bathroom and no hot water - just a cold water tap. Indeed, the first house I bought was like that!

We went out into the yard to the privy when we needed the toilet and we bathed once a week in a zinc bath in front of the living room fire.

Yet these were the years when much of the world in our school atlases was coloured pink to show us the extent of the British Empire. Many of us grew up with the clear impression that our combination of Empire and the Christian religion demonstrated that we were superior to any other nation on earth! No wonder so many people hated us so much. Fortunately for us the Americans have now taken over the position of most hated nation, although we have earned plenty of dislike for our support of America.

It seems incredible now, but I grew up believing that whatever Britain stood for was always right and good. As a result, whatever setbacks we might endure along the way, we would always win through and come out on top in the end. The outcome of the Second World War seemed to underline and confirm these ridiculous views.

They didn't last very long. I was already feeling uncomfortable enough about the whole concept of empire to be glad when India achieved independence in 1947 and when virtually the whole of the empire followed suit over the following 20 years. And yet it still came as something of a shock when one of my daughters said,

"Our country has done nothing in my lifetime of which I can be proud."

My first reaction was that she was absolutely right, and then I remembered that, thanks to a dodgy goal, we had won the world soccer cup! There are other good things that have happened in her lifetime too, and rather more in mine. There was the post-war establishment of the welfare state. There was the abolition of hanging and the creation of the Open University. There was the liberalisation of the law carried through by labour and the liberals when Roy Jenkins was Home Secretary. And women have made significant advances, many of them enshrined in law.

As a result, although I often despair of my country I still feel that it is a pretty good country in which to live. And in material and technological terms I wonder at all the changes that have taken place.

WEEK 49

20,000 Homes

I was driving home after visiting a bereaved family and I found myself totting up the number of homes I must have visited in my lifetime. 20,000 is almost certainly an exaggeration but I must have visited between 15 and 20 thousand homes all told.

Most of those homes have been in this country but not all of them. I have been in the homes of some of the poorest people in the world and I have visited the homes of a few people who are or were seriously wealthy. I remember one man saying to me,

"Do you know, I've never had to worry about money in my life."

There can't be too many people who can say that.

So I've visited houses that were palatial and houses that were made of mud and a rough thatch, where people had so few possessions that you could easily put them and the family on a bullock cart.

As I thought about all these different homes the first thing that struck me very forcibly was that I have almost always been comfortable. I don't mean physically. When bugs are biting your bum you are not too comfortable physically! I mean that I have always been made to feel at home.

The more I think about that, the more astonishing it seems to me to be. It also led me to think about exceptions. There aren't many.

I visited one man who lived alone and who was ashamed of his neglect of his mother. He was so guilt-ridden that our whole time together was distinctly uncomfortable. I visited another man who had been at odds with his sisters for years. They wanted a reconciliation and had asked me to go and to intercede with him. He was adamant that he would never speak to them again. It was not a comfortable occasion.

The only other times when I have felt uncomfortable, and they have been very few, have been in homes of people with a rigid or dogmatic kind of religion. In such homes I sometimes feel as if I am sitting on a bed of nails. The house feels unwelcoming and cold and its occupants have all their defensive barriers in place. They are determined to keep me at arms' length. Yet even in these homes it has often proved possible to overcome every initial awkwardness and hostility and to find a path forward with some measure of mutual respect, understanding, and above all, simple friendliness.

That fact leads me to the second thing which struck me on that journey home. It is amazing how often my visits to people are visits full of laughter. And that is doubly amazing when you recognise the fact that an awful lot of my visits have been to people in the darkest hours of their lives. Yet there always seems to be laughter. It is incredible and wonderful and true. Almost always we can find things to smile about. Life is so often so serious, and this book of mine in which I have been *letting off steam* has also been serious, but we seem to find it quite impossible to be serious all the time.

When you talk to people who have been in love with one another for a long time, almost always they will speak of the way in which one of them makes the other one laugh. Laughter is the best medicine and fortunately there is a great deal of it about.

As a boy I was aware of the reputation of cockneys and the same reputation of British soldiers for a cheeky, sparrow-like cheerfulness. It was a cheerfulness in spite of all that life threw at them. As boys we learned that a boy scout *smiles and whistles under all difficulties*. The amazing fact is that people do.

WEEK 50

A Spirit Of Thankfulness

As this year of *letting off steam* draws to a close I have felt
increasingly that I wanted to end positively. Sadly I have to
warn you that there is a cold blast still to come! But not
this week:

On a cold, dark, wet winter's morning I sat reading a piece
by H L Gee where he was telling us to be thankful to God
for all the lovely things summer offers in the countryside:

"the blue dome of heaven, white clouds with sunshine on
them, the sweep of distant hills, meadows where the cattle
move slowly amid warm fragrance, rivers of shining silver,
so cool in the sultry afternoon, open leaves and smiling
flowers, the majesty of trees, the promise of ripening fields,
the circling of swallows, the music of the lark climbing
high."

There is no need to conjecture a God in order to be thankful for all of these things. One of our local clergy claims
that belief in God gives you a heightened sense of the value
of them all. He just makes the claim without offering any
evidence at all. It is a claim I reject. When I believed in God
I loved the countryside. Now that I do not believe in God I
love the countryside. There is no difference at all. There is
no need for religion at all. Any one of us can cultivate a
spirit of thankfulness.

Thinking these thoughts on my cold, dark, wet winter's
morning I looked at my wife sitting reading quietly in the
armchair beside my own and I thought, those of us without
religion have just as much to be thankful for as those who
turn to their gods. Nor do we have to look very far before
we find people to be thankful to and people to be thankful
for. I remembered my brother speaking of his digs in

Kilburn many, many years ago. When the family sat down at the table for their meals as people used to do long, long ago, they always began their meals with *grace.* The first time he heard it, as a Christian, he was somewhat taken aback:

"For what we are about to receive may we be truly grateful to our mother."

No need for the Lord to make us thankful. Irreligious people know where gratitude is due. We may feel that such formality is unnecessary but there is no doubt that such a spirit of thankfulness, a thankfulness frequently expressed and given to those to whom it is due, is an essential part of a truly happy life.

WEEK 51

Christmas

Throughout the year 2000 many churches had a large poster outside saying something like: "Jesus Christ was born 2000 years ago. Come and worship him." Some churches still haven't taken the message down!

Recently the local churches' newsletter came and I searched it for a Christmas message. The only one I could find was, Christmas is the birthday of Jesus. Come and worship him on his birthday."

One of the things Christianity is supposed to stand for is truth. Yet neither of the statements in those first two paragraphs is true. If Jesus was born at all it was probably between 6 and 4 BCE. Nobody knows for sure when or where he was born or what time of year it was. At the time of his birth it was too unimportant for anyone to notice it!

But the church is guilty of worse than untruths. It is guilty of theft! This is true of most if not all Christian festivals. Having no specific dates of their own, the church took over dates which were important to other people in order to Christianise dates which had a real significance for many non-Christians. Late December was of immense importance to all sorts of people, notably to Jews and Romans. Christians simply took it over in order to place their own imprint on it.

Recognising this, and recognising the simple fact that England is no longer a country with one predominant religion, a national magazine asked three people to express what late December meant: a Jew, a Muslim and a Christian. I read all three. All that the Christian, a clergyman, could tell us was that for him this was a very busy time of year!

But there is still worse to come. The stories of angels and shepherds and wise men may make pleasant enough nativity plays but just stop and think about the story of the virgin birth for a moment.

No doubt at the time it seemed important to match all those pagan stories about gods mating with humans. But what it has really done is to call in to question the value and importance of ordinary human sexual intercourse. Paul picked up on it right away in one of his New Testament letters where he states that marriage is only for those who are too weak or too passionate to be celibate. And the Catholic Church throughout the ages has followed him, treating virginity as if it was something special and raising the mother of Jesus almost to the status of another god.

The story of the virgin birth has led the church to treat sex as something dirty, surrounded by taboos, instead of as something that can be lovely, pure, holy and one of the supremely wonderful experiences available to human beings.

Set on one side all the pretty stories and there are only three Christian messages at Christmas that are of any significance at all. For an atheist the claim that "the promises of God are true" is meaningless, so I'm going to concentrate on the other two.

If the first of them were true it would be mind-bending and would DEMAND our attention. Yet I haven't heard so much as a whisper of it this Christmas. If I were a Christian I would proclaim it above all else. If people found that it was beyond belief I would be saddened but at least I would know that I had confronted people with one of the most momentous claims that Christianity makes, the claim that God became a human being and that he did so because he loves us. "The Word" (=Jesus) "became flesh and dwelt among us."

This claim is expressed beautifully at the beginning of John's Gospel. If there were a God and if this claim were true it would perhaps be the greatest claim made by any religion. It is almost beyond imagining. Even now it is intellectually exciting and can stir the emotions of believers very deeply indeed.

Does the church no longer dare to make the claim? Does it no longer believe it? Certainly, this Christmas I haven't heard a whisper of it.

I can understand Christians avoiding the other Christmas message which has to do with "peace on earth and goodwill among men." The Christian church has so often been associated with anything but "peace and goodwill." In its own divisions and hostilities it gives the lie to the message it is supposed to proclaim. Throughout its history it has been a divisive rather than a unifying force, both amongst Christians and between Christians and non-Christians. Jesus never spoke a truer word than his "I did not come to bring peace but a sword."

If I were a Christian I would want to condemn Christian failures in peace and goodwill; I would want to urge Christians to take up the challenge and be peacemakers/keepers; and I would want to carry that message into the world at large - a goal towards which anyone can work regardless of race or religion.

New Beginnings

One Christmas or birthday when I was a boy I was given a wax tablet. We used them to write or draw on. When the tablet was full or when we wanted to begin again there was a bar which we passed over the tablet to 'wipe the slate clean.' The bar erased what we had done and we were able to begin again.

But as the tablet grew older it grew harder to erase them completely. And as we tried to write something new there was an increasing danger that what we had done before would show through.

Life is like that.

There are times when we want to make a new start and we always can. But it grows harder as we grow older, and it is harder still to erase the marks of the past. But new beginnings are ALWAYS possible. Whether we are trying to pick ourselves up after making disastrous mistakes in life, or whether we are trying to begin again after bereavement, or whether we are trying to escape from an addiction and begin anew, a new start IS ALWAYS POSSIBLE. Possible, not easy, but possible, and the longer we continue our new life, the less painful those marks from the past become. But if we are seeking to make a new beginning, whether for a new year, or at any other time in our lives, what are the things that will matter?

It seems to me that the best place to start is with simple human friendship.

No two people have the same ideas or ideals. Nobody else stands precisely where I stand. It would be desperately uncomfortable if they did. But there are masses of people

140

who stand close enough for me to be reached by them, and for me to be able to reach out to them in simple, ordinary human friendship.

That seems to me to be more important than almost anything else in life. More than anything else in life we need to be able to get on with other people and they need to be able to get on with us. That means that we have to be able to accept them as they are and that they need to be able to accept us as we are without either of us wanting to make a change to the other. So many marriages come unstuck because one partner wants to remake the other into the ideal dream person he or she had always wanted to marry.

None of us is ideal. We are not the stuff of dreams. We are creatures of flesh and blood with our own thoughts and feelings, thoughts and feelings which no one else can fully share. Whether you happen to be a Hindu or a Jew, a Christian or a Muslim is irrelevant. Whether you happen to be wealthy or poor, male or female, black or white or all shades in between; whatever your class or caste; none of these things matter. They are all irrelevant.

All that we need is enough common ground for us to be friends. Epicurus taught us that friendship can and should be unlimited. It can cross ALL barriers. It can be the one unifying force that can hold us all together within the one human family. It is probably the ONLY unifying force.

It will be clear that I have no time for evangelism. Our task is not to try to convert other people so that they become what we are. Our task is simply to hold out the hand of friendship knowing that everything else can flow from that.

Whether we are looking to continue the lives we are living in the best possible way, or looking to make a genuine new start after personal disaster, there is no better place to start than in ordinary human friendship.